Battleground

YPRES 1

MESSINES

Battleground Europe

YPRES 1914

MESSINES

Nigel Cave
and Jack Sheldon

Series Editor
Nigel Cave

Pen & Sword
MILITARY

Dedication

Dedicated to the memory of Colonel Terence Arthur Cave CBE, 1923–2015; he took the 14-year-old Nigel Cave to the Western Front in the summer of 1968, thirty-one years after his own visit with his veteran father in 1937, when he, too, was 14. Together, Nigel and Terry made some thirty visits 'over there' between 1981 and 2009.

First published in Great Britain in 2015 by
Pen & Sword Military
An imprint of
Pen & Sword Books Ltd
47 Church Street   Barnsley
South Yorkshire   S70 2AS

Copyright © Nigel Cave and Jack Sheldon

ISBN 978 178159 201 4

Typeset in Times New Roman by Chic Graphics

Printed and bound in England by
CPI Group (UK) Ltd., Croydon, CR0 4YY

Pen & Sword Books Ltd incorporates the imprints of
Pen & Sword Archaeology, Atlas, Aviation, Battleground, Discovery,
Family History, History, Maritime, Military, Naval, Politics,
Railways, Select, Social History, Transport, True Crime,
Claymore Press, Frontline Books, Leo Cooper, Praetorian Press,
Remember When, Seaforth Publishing and Wharncliffe.

For a complete list of Pen & Sword titles please contact
PEN & SWORD BOOKS LIMITED
47 Church Street, Barnsley, South Yorkshire, S70 2AS, England
E-mail: enquiries@pen-and-sword.co.uk
Website: www.pen-and-sword.co.uk

CONTENTS

Introductory Comments

Note: Because the repeated use of (Cavalry) after a divisional or brigade number becomes tiresome, except when it is necessary for purposes of clarity, it is not used in this account, which more than is usual concerns cavalry formations. The British used three cavalry divisions during the Battle of Ypres 1914: 1st, 2nd and 3rd.

The move of the bulk of the BEF from the Aisne to the northern part of the allied armies has been covered in outline in Langemarck, the first of this trilogy of books on the Battle of Ypres 1914. This, the second book in the trilogy, is largely concerned with what is officially called the Battle of Messines 1914, 12 October – 2 November; but not exclusively so, as it extends to the fighting west of the Comines-Ypres railway line and up to the south of the Menin Road and well beyond the formal closure date of Messines 1914.

The area covered by this book is chiefly remembered for the fighting on 31st October/1st November on Messines Ridge, in particular the contribution of the London Scottish, the first infantry unit of the Territorial Army to be engaged in battle and in which it performed well. As the reader will discover, we hope, there was a lot more to the fighting than that.

The early fighting predominantly involved the cavalry of both sides; the British were later to be joined by elements of the Indian Army Corps, making its first (and for its infantry, its only) appearance in the area of Ypres. It is also, along with the northern part of the Salient, a place where the French army made a notable and decisive intervention, in this case in the fighting of November 1914.

Almost all of the ground covered must qualify as being the most tranquil part of that part of Belgium that is associated with 'Wipers'. Although woods may have expanded or, more often, contracted, the terrain has largely escaped the development associated with the dynamic economic expansion that is a characteristic of western Flanders over the last thirty years or more. Roads run, more or less, along their old course and they are often not much wider than they were in 1914 (although they are rather smoother now). It is one of the less encumbered parts of the battlefield and makes a visit to it all the more rewarding as a consequence.

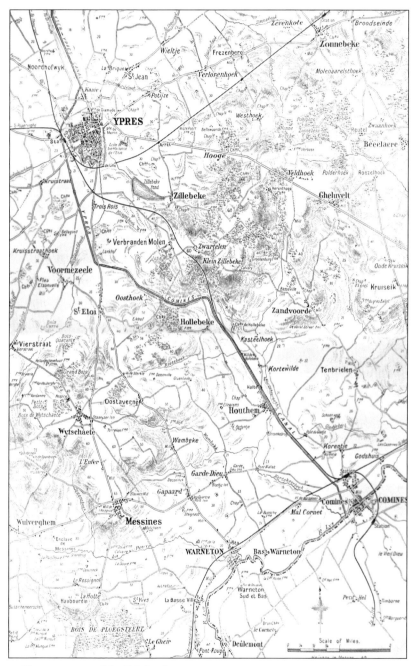

The area covered by this book.

7

Chapter One

Cavalry Operations:
The lead up to the main action
16–29 October

 On 18 October Allenby's Cavalry Corps, which had been created on 9 October, comprising two under establishment divisions, the 1st and the 2nd, held the line from east of Ploegsteert Wood in the south to Zandvoorde to the north. On the Corps' right was 4th Division (III Corps) and on the left 7th Division (IV Corps).

In an ideal world, the established strength of a British cavalry division was some 9,250 men, comprising four brigades, each with three cavalry regiments (compared with an infantry brigade, which had four battalions); it also had artillery (RHA), engineers, signal squadrons, field ambulances and supply columns. A 1914 British cavalry division, in theory, was twice as big as a French cavalry division and almost twice as large as its German equivalent. A full strength British infantry division, by comparison, had approximately 18,000 men, a German one 17,000 men and a French one 15,000 men.

Edmund Allenby.

In 1914 a British cavalry regiment at full strength had 549 men, of whom twenty six were officers – that is approximately half the size of an infantry battalion although there was roughly parity in the number of officers. Each regiment was split into three squadrons of 150 men each, commanded by a major; and each squadron into four troops of thirty men and a couple of sergeants, commanded by a lieutenant or second lieutenant. Since the cavalry fought dismounted at Ypres, it is important to be clear about the significant difference in rifle strength between a cavalry regiment and an infantry battalion; the former, if holding a trench line, would be further diminished by the large number of men who were required to look after the horses.

In fact at this stage 1st (Cavalry) Division, commanded by Major General H de B de Lisle, only had two brigades and six regiments

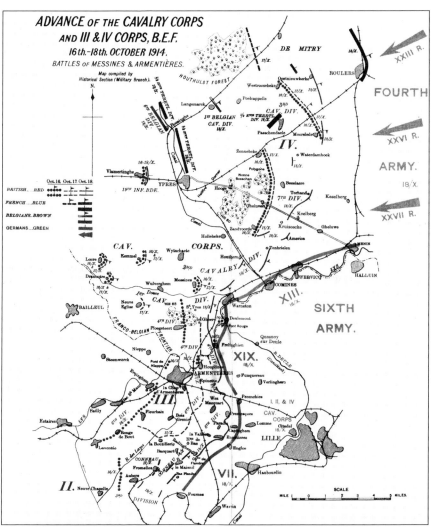

ADVANCE OF THE CAVALRY CORPS AND III & IV CORPS, B.E.F. 16th.-18th. OCTOBER 1914. BATTLES OF MESSINES & ARMENTIÈRES.

Beauvoir de Lisle.

Hubert Gough.

(another arrived right at the end of October) and 2nd (Cavalry) Division, commanded by Major General H Gough, had three brigades and nine regiments. Another under strength cavalry division (the 3rd, Major General J Byng) with only two brigades and six regiments (until 20 November, when another brigade was added), served initially with Rawlinson's IV Corps but was transferred on 24 October and came under the Cavalry Corps on 25 October; even then it was more often than not 'lent' to Haig's I Corps.

Julian Byng.

The diary of Lieutenant Trevor Horn gives some insight into these early days of the cavalry fighting south of Ypres; he was with the machine guns of 16/Lancers (3 Brigade). The Lancers were largely instrumental in the removal of the German cavalry from Mont des Cats, south west of Poperinghe, on 12 October, an attack in which Prince Max of Hesse was killed. Horn notes that, during the night of the 12th, the horses were all crammed into a big yard in the monastery (which today still dominates the top of the hill), whilst 'the poor old monks worked like slaves for everyone and talking like mad – I suppose their Trappist vows did not apply on an occasion like this'. The Lancers moved south over the next couple of days and by the evening of the 14th were billeted for the night near Wytschaete. On the 15th they went forward to reconnoitre Warneton, which was found to be occupied by the Germans, though the cavalry did manage to break into the south west corner. At this stage the British were digging in north of the canal and the Germans were doing likewise to the south of it.

16/Lancers at Hollebeke Chateau, soon after their arrival in the Ypres area.

On **16 October**:

About 10 am was ordered to rejoin D Squadron and went back to same place as previous day, sending one [machine] gun into the village. About 3.30 pm [Brigadier] *General Gough* [commanding 2nd (Cavalry) Division – he was formally promoted to major general on 26 September, along with about ten others] *and Colonel Greenly rode up and I directed them to where Onslow was in the village, as they wanted to see the enemy's trenches etc., on the far side of the canal. About 4.30 pm E Battery* [Royal Horse Artillery] *went up the SW end of Warneton and came into action. It was then decided that we should attack the centre of the village, which was barricaded. One of my* [machine] *guns had been placed on a roof overlooking the barricade, a hole being knocked through the tiles. The plan was that one gun of E Battery was to be manhandled up a side street and then quickly pushed around the corner and fired at the barricade, under the cover of my MG firing from the roof; and then one troop of C Squadron was to rush the barricade, backed up if necessary by the rest of C Squadron and half of A Squadron. It was quite dark by the time all this was arranged.*

We were all standing along the sides of the street, with a certain amount of odd sniping going on towards the village centre, when the gun went off – I've never heard such a row – a deafening crack and then the breaking and falling of glass all over and round one, as of course every window was broken to pieces, and most of the houses were three stories high. Three shells were fired and then C Squadron rushed and took the barricade… A good deal of shooting was going on from windows and doorways: it was pitch dark and one couldn't tell where it was coming from or who was shooting, as one could not see from the flash from a rifle whether it was being fired towards one or from one, also wherever the bullet struck a brick or stone there was a flash. On reaching the centre square there was another barricade down a right hand street leading down to the canal: one MG was placed at the corner so that it could fire at this, and the man could lean round and look occasionally but could fire it from behind the corner, merely putting his hand out to press the button. I took the other gun across to the opposite side of the square, each of us being covered in turn as we ran across by the gun already in position. Corporal Willis and a patrol of four men had been sent across just in front to work down towards the

11

barricade – it was lucky for us, as two men were shot from a doorway on the other side of the street and, if one of my men had been there instead, it would probably have meant losing the gun. We put the gun up in the same way as the other one.

All this time there was odd shooting going on, and all the side roads were being barricaded and picketed. A big house was on fire on our side of the square, making any movement visible, but luckily one had also caught fire near their barricade and they couldn't move much without being seen. Suddenly a 'Verey' [sic] flare light came over and dropped almost into the square, lighting up everything as though it was daylight: it was our first experience of them, and one could see everyone crouching as close to the walls as possible, wondering what was going to happen next; personally I thought when it touched the ground there would be an awful explosion, but of course nothing of the sort happened.

... The next item was a machine gun opening fire from their barricade onto my other gun, which promptly replied, and it was the most extraordinary but horrid sight to see these two MGs like a couple of angry cats spitting at each other not more than twenty five yards apart, sparks flying wherever the bullets hit the cobbles or the walls and the noise of course being deafening. Thank goodness our gun had been set up and laid when not under fire, whereas their gun had been brought up under fire and consequently badly aimed, the shots (as I heard afterwards) going about five feet wide, otherwise Corporal Brookes must have been riddled with bullets, as we had only managed to raise two mattresses for protection.

Instructed to retire, the regiment left Warneton by 11.30 pm,

... all except the Doctor (Johnson), who remained behind with the wounded in the hospital. What an awful time he must have had being left behind in the dark, knowing he was bound to be taken prisoner next morning, or failing that being shelled by either one side or the other.

Johnson was duly taken prisoner, but was repatriated – something quite common for medical officers – later on in the war, in December 1915. There were a very large number of RAMC officers taken prisoner in these first months of the war – certainly when the size of the BEF at that time is taken into account – not far off fifty of them; such figures for the

RAMC would not be repeated until the German offensives of spring 1918.

The regiment then returned to Messines:

> ... hadn't got far before getting both limbers well into a ditch. Flares were now going all over the village, and the Germans began to shell along the Warneton-Messines road, evidently thinking a big attack was going to be made on it. Reached Messines about 12.30 am and put up at the Institute Royale. Everyone dead beat. Hope we don't do any more street fighting in the dark, as it doesn't seem our job, not knowing when or where one may be attacked from next. What the inhabitants must have gone through heaven knows, as there were any number of women and children hiding in the cellars, the men having all been taken away previously to dig the German trenches.

The skirmishing continued into the next day. 3/Hussars (4 Brigade) came into the line on **17 October** and relieved men of 3 Brigade in front of Gapaard (where regimental headquarters were situated) and were greeted by snipers. They held a line of some two miles, roughly along the line of the Messines-Comines road, with the Germans in occupation of Warneton, a kilometre to the south. By noon they came under attack from Warneton; supported by J Battery RHA they were able to deal with this. An attempt about that time was made to make contact with 5 Brigade on its left. The troop ran into trouble as it crossed the Comines Canal bridge north west of Comines station.

3/Hussars, passing through Flêtre, on 13 October on their way to Flanders, meet up with 1/R Irish Rifles.

The advanced point of the troop and the officer, Lieutenant J Eliot [subsequently to win the MC and be severely wounded on 30 October], *crossed the canal bridge to the cover of a farm, and signalled to the troop to close up. As soon as the troop was well on the bridge a German machine gun opened on it from a house near the station* [in fact it was in the church tower, near the station]. *Two horses were killed on the bridge and blocked it. Those on its western side managed to retire to cover, but the officer and men with him had to cross back as best they could... The troop finally took up a position on the road just west of the Kortekeer Beek. All the advanced troops proceeded to entrench themselves with whatever implements they could find in the vicinity.*

On **18 October**, in line with the allied plan, Sir John French, commanding the BEF, ordered his forces to advance eastwards; the Cavalry Corps engaged the Germans along a line roughly from Deûlémont (east of Ploegsteert Wood) to Tenbrielen, a couple of miles north of Comines. It made no progress and already the German line around Ypres, albeit unknown to the allies, was rapidly thickening up as the Germans prepared their own attempt to sweep through what had been the open flank of both armies. The Corps did very little on **19 October**; whilst it faced significant problems on **20 October**.

The *Official History* [*OH*] states that on that date the Corps consisted of about 9,000 men – that is approximately the strength of one cavalry division at full establishment - and was covering a front of over six miles. Its men were scattered from the area of Deûlémont to as far north as the intriguingly named hamlet of America (where John Eden of 12/Lancers, Sir Anthony Eden's brother, had been killed on 17 October), south of the Menin Road. The German push comprised six cavalry divisions, consisting of about 24,000 troops and Allenby – realising by 8 am that the Germans were engaged in a general attack – gradually withdrew his divisions back to preselected positions. The 1st Division held a line from approximately St Yves, at the north east of Ploegsteert Wood, to Messines, with 4th (Infantry) Division on its right; whilst 2nd Division continued the line north eastwards, to Houthem and across the canal at Kortewilde, where it met the right flank of the 7th Division. The history of 3 (King's Own) Hussars notes:

From the early hours of the 20th the enemy in our front showed signs of activity, and shots were exchanged with snipers who had come forward. At about 10 am the right troop of the left squadron was heavily attacked by infantry, and both the posts which it

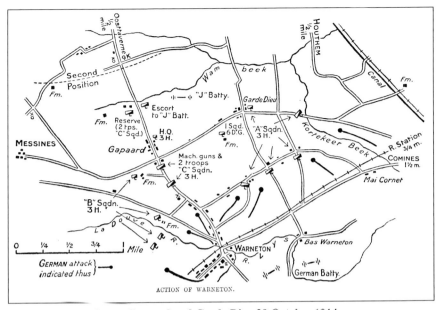

Cavalry Action at Gapaard and Garde Dieu 20 October 1914.

supplied had to retire on Garde Dieu. Almost simultaneously a heavy attack began to be made from Warneton against the right squadron. Soon the whole front of the Regiment was engaged. A German battery opened and J Battery and another RHA battery nearer Messines, both firing indirect, came into action.

There were soon calls for assistance from both flanks, and the two reserve troops were sent from the centre to B Squadron on the right, while a squadron of the Carabiniers [ie 6/Dragoon Guards] that had arrived in support was sent to the left centre. There only remained now one squadron of Carabiniers, which was to escort J Battery. Gapaard was heavily shelled, and the horses there had to be led to the valley of the Wambeek, north of the village. Crash through the roof of the village inn came a high explosive shell, and out through its door, 'pouff!' came Monsieur le Capitaine, the French interpreter, hurried somewhat by another immediate crash in the inn yard. Garde Dieu, too, was heavily shelled throughout the day. The position, with desperate fighting everywhere, was held on until after 4 pm, when it became clear that the Regiment must retire. The dogged determination of the men, heavily shelled throughout the day, and exposed, by nature of the small isolated posts (unavoidable because of the few in numbers and the extended front), to enfilade fire everywhere, was of no avail. There was no haste, however: the squadrons held and, disputing foot by foot every yard of ground, did the dismounted hussars fall back to their horses. An officer had been sent to select the next position to retire upon. To the Oostaverne Ridge [in the area of Wambeke] *the battery and its supporting squadrons fell back. Messages were sent to the flank squadrons to retire on the ridge and the centre and Headquarters slowly withdrew. The retirement was carried out in capital order and, as the centre squadron reaching the ninth kilometre stone on the* [Ypres] *road crossing the ridge, it was found that 5 Brigade had been brought up and was hastily entrenching the position.*

The day's work for 3/Hussars was not completed, however. Reorganised north of the ridge, relatively secure on the reverse slope south of the Wambeke, orders were received at 6.15 pm to extend the line from the right of 6/DG (Carabiniers), west of Wambeke, towards Messines, filling in the gap between 6/DG and the Composite Regiment (formed from elements of the two regiments of the Household Cavalry), who were supposed to be covering the eastern side of Messines. This process was not easy – B Squadron had been left as a cover for the withdrawal in a valley north west of Gapaard and had to be recalled, whilst the left flank of 6/DG had to be found, all in the dark.

Lieutenant Colonel AA Kennedy, CO of 3/Hussars, pictured later in the war.

This was a most hazardous but necessary movement. It was already quite dark, and the locality was within a mile of the line reached by the enemy some two hours previously. Further, there was no certainty that the Composite Regiment had retired by the eastern side of Messines. After successfully hitting off the flank of the Carabiniers and recalling B Squadron by a ride across country in the dark, the advance was continued by compass bearing towards Messines. Roads shown on the map did not exist, but after stumbling along through heavy mud for another hour, a farm was reached near a windmill [Blauwen Molen], *where the Composite Regiment's left should certainly have rested. The farm was at once occupied, pickets thrown out, and horses concealed behind the buildings, whilst reconnaissance was pushed farther forward to gain touch with the Composite Regiment, but unsuccessfully. It was now about 8.30 pm and, just as the reconnaissance party returned, a squadron of the Composite Regiment was met, having come up from the rear of the Regiment.*

The Regiment suffered three killed or died of wounds and twenty or so wounded, including five officers, with two men missing (presumably they became PoWs) in the time they held the line here between 17 and 20 October 1914.

Once in their new positions the cavalry busily engaged in digging themselves in and fending off any German attempts to move forward. The *OH* quotes the historian of the German Guard Cavalry Division:

The enemy drew back, it is true, but only to his main position just east of Messines. From there he kept the ground in front under such an annihilating fire that our riflemen had to remain lying down 600 metres from the [La Potterie] *farm.*

5 Brigade, which included 20/Hussars, was positioned that evening to 4 Brigade's right, to the east of the Oosttaverne – Warneton road. It had had a busy couple of days; on the afternoon of the 18th it had been ordered to capture and hold Tenbrielen and then on the 19th moved to America. The task was to cover the Division's left flank as it advanced on Menin (see *Langemarck*), but that advance had to be abandoned and the 20th had a fairly uneventful day. On the 20th they returned to America, with the same orders as for the 19th – but it was far less quiet. Patrols were sent out to

Lieutenant Colonel Edwards, CO 20/Hussars.

Werviq, where they made contact with the Germans. Rather ominously, artillery fire from both sides increased significantly. However, that afternoon the regiment moved hurriedly to the Oosttaverne area, instructed to support the withdrawal of 4 Brigade, the latter under attack from Warneton.

5 Brigade's position started with Greys on the right, astride the road, in contact with 4 Brigade; 12/Lancers were on the left and 20/Hussars in the centre. All were instructed to dig in but, as the regimental history noted: 'Alas! The entrenching tools had been jettisoned for the pursuit over the Marne'. Lieutenant Hall described his experience:

Spent most of the night digging a trench with the aid of a broken plate, mess tins and knives and forks. Bayonets were also used,

17

and a few spades were collected at Oosttaverne. The inhabitants, before parting with these, were insistent in demanding that they should be returned when we had finished with them! Poor devils! This was their first experience of war. They knew more about it a fortnight later, I expect. The sappers from the Field Troop did what they could for us and their help was invaluable. We dug all night.

However, the light of the morning of the 21st showed that the position was not a good one; a new one was taken up, further behind, which turned out to be an improvement all around – they occupied a line behind the crest of the ridge and yet had good fields of fire. Mind you, the knives and forks had to go to work again!

Further north on the **20th**, 4/Hussars (3 Brigade) was brought up in the morning to the Hollebeke area, one that was to become keenly disputed in the days ahead, and to dig a line through the village.

We were very busy digging, employing a good many civilians to help and using civilian tools. ... We made the mistake in these early days of building overhead cover to the trenches [which remained quite a common practice amongst the French for some time], *which made them far too conspicuous, as we were to learn on 30 and 31 October.*

The next passage from the regimental history underlines two major problems during this battle: the paucity of troops and the lack of anything like the sort of line that became common after it; and the poor communications set up. The latter was a matter of technology, lack of signallers, a changing front and the dependence on line. In their place were despatch riders, staff officers and regimental liaison officers sent to pass on information about a particular situation. Here the professionalism of the BEF paid off, in the sense that officers of all ranks seem to have been capable of

The humble cyclist could be a crucial means of communication in the war of movement.

grasping a situation and reporting it as accurately as they could. It needs a complete change of mind-set for observers of the Great War to understand the fighting at this stage of the war, as it is so antithetical to everything else that happened in it until 1918 – and even then signals communications were far better, at least potentially, than then. In passing, it might be added, without horses and a solid corpus of men and officers who could ride well, it is a certainty that the British would have lost First Ypres – not to mention the general manoeuvrability of the cavalry divisions. Motorbike despatch riders existed, but many crucial communications required speed and the road and ground conditions were more often than not such that there was little possibility that motor cycles could be as efficient or as speedy as a man on horseback could be.

At noon [20th] *orders were received to prepare for a retirement in case 5 Brigade* [on the right] *were forced in. There was some uncertainty throughout this period as to the position of other bodies of troops, and it was very rare to be informed of the movements of other units, which we had to find out for ourselves. For instance, in this case we were not informed where 5 Brigade was, and were ourselves unable to locate it; it was not easy, therefore, to conform to their movements* [!]. *Colonel Howell* [the CO] *was, however, indefatigable in obtaining information as to neighbouring troops and, thanks to his energy, the regiment was usually better informed than most as to the situation.*

Over on the right, 11 (Prince Albert's Own) Hussars, part of 1 Brigade (Brigadier General Briggs, of 1st [Cavalry] Division), had a busy time on the 20th as well. It has an outstanding regimental history. On 20 October they were moved forward from their overnight billets around Petit Pont, some two miles north west of Ploegsteert and which had been used for the purpose – along with nights in Kemmel – since 14 October. In the morning they moved to Ploegsteert Wood, but were brought into Ploegsteert itself at 2 pm to act as a mobile reserve for 12 Brigade (4th Division), under pressure to the east; they were not, as events unfolded, needed in the end. However, at 4 pm 1 Brigade was ordered up to the crossroads to the west of Hill 63, from where there was:

... a good view of the country to the north; from the crossroads the ground sloped gently down to the Douve stream and rose again on the further side of the stream up to the village of Messines, which stands in a somewhat commanding position. The ground in this shallow trough of the Douve was bare and open, the only

cover being afforded by farm buildings and by a few hedgerows. Across this ground, when the regiment arrived at the cross-roads, some Household Cavalry [the Composite Regiment of the Household Cavalry, which consisted of one squadron each from 1st and 2nd Life Guards and a squadron of Royal Horse Guards] *of 4 Brigade could be seen retiring at a gallop towards Messines.*

By 4.30 pm, on Briggs' orders, 11/Hussars was advancing eastwards from the main Messines-Ploegsteert road south of the Douve, 2/DG (the Bays) north of it and 5/DG moved into Messines itself – fortunately, as it happened, because it found it vacated by 4 Brigade. Just before dark contact was made with the Germans. 11/Hussars established a line a couple of hundred yards forward of La Douve Farm, where Regimental HQ based itself. During a rather wet night – and after the tool carts were found – and in the early morning, with benefit of daylight, a new line was established; the Germans did the same about a thousand yards away.

Lieutenant Colonel T Pitman, CO of 11/Hussars, pictured later in the war.

21 October saw the Cavalry Corps under consistent attack; to the south, by the end of the day, 1st Division had shortened its line to the Douve, with units of 4th Division taking over the positions south of the river to Ploegsteert Wood. Otherwise it had fended off German cavalry attacks.

To the north east of Messines the line was held by the Composite Regiment of the Household Cavalry. Surgeon Major Cowie's diary notes:

Regiment holding trenches on high ground a mile east by north of Messines on the Messines road, by a windmill, which stood on a round grassed mound; the mill itself was entirely of wood resting on a single pedestal, also of wood. The Germans occasionally shelled this mill. One of the shells (shrapnel) wounded the CO [Lieutenant Colonel EB Cook] *on the leg, Captain Astor elbow, Corporal Moore stomach, Trooper Tobin back, and another. Otherwise a quiet day. A light ambulance wagon was brought up past the farm at the rear of the position and the wounded were removed to Wytschaete where they were transferred to a motor ambulance.* [Colonel Cook died in early November, back in England.]

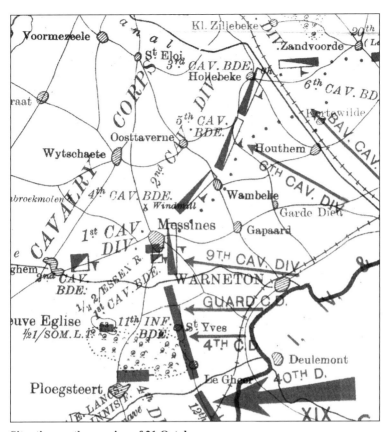

Situation on the evening of 21 October.

Further north, on 2nd (Cavalry) Division's front, attacks launched at about 9.30 am forced 3 Brigade out of their trenches and the hamlet of Kortewilde, just east of the canal, a couple of hours later. For whatever reason, divisional instructions relating to lines of retreat were taken as an order to withdraw immediately to St Eloi. The Brigade therefore abandoned Hollebeke and its chateau, which was about half a mile east of the village, having first advised 20 Brigade, 7th Division, on its left. Gough reacted by ordering the line Messines-Oostaverne-Hollebeke to be held and the village was reoccupied, though not at this stage the chateau; at the end of the day the lines were a considerable distance apart – maybe 2,500 yards in the north down to a thousand yards in the south of the Corps' position. To help to deal with the pressure on his right flank, IV Corps (Lieutenant General Rawlinson) sent his 3rd (Cavalry) Division to Zillebeke, with 6 Brigade, late that evening, occupying the practically vacant section of the British line between Zandvoorde and the canal, over to the west.

Extracts from 4/Hussar's history have already given a good indication of just how complicated things were for the very overstretched Cavalry Corps on the 20th; things around Hollebeke were not much better the following day:

On the 21st all were expecting an enemy attack at any moment, while our situation was far from satisfactory, as there were apparently no troops between Hollebeke and Zandvoorde, and the position of 5th [Royal Irish, 3 Brigade] *Lancers was uncertain. As soon as it got light the situation began to clear up, and at 9.30 am 5/Lancers were astride the canal to our front at the lock and windmill. Our left was still in the air, so A Squadron, Captain Pragnell, was ordered to Klein Zillebeke to fill the gap.*

No sooner was he clear of the village [ie Hollebeke] *than heavy field gun fire opened on it. The first shells struck the Curé's house, just evacuated by Headquarters, and the estaminet was the next target, Lieutenant Cripps and a cyclist being wounded there. The firing increased, but was directed almost entirely against buildings in the higher portion of the village and not all against the trenches in front of it where out men lay. This was probably due to the care with which they had been sited by Colonel Howell* [killed, as a brigadier general, in October 1916 and buried at Varennes], *and to his strict orders against movement near them by day. 5/Lancers now withdrew from our front and German infantry began to advance from Kortewilde,*

5th Lancers on the move near Wytschaete.

some crossing the canal and advancing along the west bank, while cavalry were seen farther to the east. There was probably a whole brigade of German infantry advancing along both sides of the canal by 11 am and B Squadron and one machine gun – and especially one advanced troop under Captain Brooke – had some fair targets, though the country was rather blind. Our gunners were put on to some targets and did some execution; whilst 6 (Cavalry) brigade guns, coming up north of the canal, near the Ypres road, were also given targets by us.

This appeared to steady the German advance, and by 12.30 pm we were feeling pretty comfortable and felt we had the situation well in hand, more especially as a hundred cyclists [almost certainly 7 Cyclist Company, 7th Division] *had now filled the gap on our left, when we were ordered to retire, first to the canal bend north of Hollebeke and then towards St Eloi. The withdrawal was gradually carried out, the enemy showing no great desire to press on in face of our fire, and by 2.30 pm we were just clear of the village. At this juncture counter-orders were received, to hold on to Hollebeke at all costs. The regiment immediately turned about and went forward to occupy its former positions. On reaching the village again, however, it was found that the enemy had occupied the chateau and the houses level with it on the west of the canal. At 3.30 pm we arranged, in*

Cavalry at rest near Hollebeke Chateau.

conjunction with 10/Hussars [6 Brigade], *on the east of the railway, to attack the chateau. 10/Hussars, however, did not attack and the Germans advanced from it instead against our B Squadron, covering the canal and railway crossings there, and by 4.15 pm the attack was becoming serious. However, the Germans shot remarkably badly; we got our guns on to them and this, combined with our rifle fire, caused their attack to die away at about 4.45 pm.*

At 6.30 pm the situation was much the same, 10/Hussars having been told to occupy the chateau if not held by the enemy. They sent patrols down, who apparently reported it held. Meanwhile our patrols found the canal crossing evacuated and B Squadron occupied it at 9 pm, sending patrols also into the chateau, which was unoccupied. However, at 12 midnight the enemy, also finding it unoccupied, reoccupied it and from there made it too uncomfortable for our men at the crossing to remain there. ... It transpired afterwards that it was some shooting by our men at the crossing which led the 10th to believe the chateau held at 9.30 pm. These shots were fired at a cow.

In fact the chateau was reoccupied by the British early on the 22nd, when it was found to be empty. Corps troops were sent up to occupy it – 200 men of 2/Munsters; however seventy were diverted to the trenches in front of Hollebeke and a platoon of them covered the canal crossing to the north. This battalion had been acting as Corps troops (ie under the direct command of the Corps commander, in this case Haig) for several weeks. On 27 August the battalion had been all but destroyed in a rearguard action at Étreux and was not sufficiently rebuilt to be able to re-enter the line as a battalion again until 8 November.

Elsewhere on the 21st it had been a busy day for the allies – I Corps was scheduled to begin an advance with the French on the left and in conjunction with IV Corps on the right; some progress was made but the attack ran full tilt into the advance by *Fourth Army*. The action here is covered, in particular, in *Ypres 1914: Langemarck*. Indeed, for the next few days, the severe fighting around Ypres was to the north of the Menin Road; relative calm to its south allowed for the gradual reinforcement of the cavalry by infantry, as horses were taken back to the rear and the men set about digging in. South of the Douve, 4th Division now covered the front to Armentières; on the 22nd the Ferozepore Brigade of the Lahore Division, from the newly arrived Indian Corps, concentrated at Bailleul, with 1/Connaught Rangers moving to Wulverghem and 57th Wilde's Rifles (the 57th) moving into the line in support of 5 Brigade, having been brought up in buses. On the 23rd 129th Baluchis (the 129th) relieved 3 Brigade and 9th Bhopal Infantry went into reserve. Although there was not much serious offensive action in this period, the Germans continued to make numerous small scale probes against the British lines and casualties were suffered; whilst the artillery was in constant action.

Although 'quiet' in the rest of the Cavalry Corps area, it would be a mistake to think this equated to a relatively comfortable time. For example, on the evening of the 21st, 3/Hussars:

... started cutting down some fences for wire entanglements (shortage of wire was a major problem), when a lot of shrapnel came bussing about us. Also rifle fire, and the support troops were called up. Bullets were flying about all over the place. It did not appear to be a night attack, but someone probably got the needle, and though they saw something, and started loosing off, then gradually everyone took it up in sympathy; as a matter of fact our men hardly fired at all.

On the 22nd Surgeon Major Cowie, with the Composite Regiment, noted:

Regiment in same position. Major Lord Crichton commanding [of the RHG; killed on 31 October and buried in Zantvoorde Military Cemetery – though his death was not confirmed until June 1916]. *Heavy firing all the early morning before daylight on left of our position. The Germans could be seen digging on the low ground on the left front. J Battery shelled them to some effect from south of Wytschaete. Murray Smith, who was left in a trench near Warneton on 20th, is in the hands of the Saxons, who are known to be gentlemen (he was taken to hospital at Lille the same day and, after doing very well for some days, died just when he was going to be moved to a private house).* [He is buried in Lille South Cemetery.]

The next day, before being relieved by the 57th, Cowie noted that, 'The wooden windmill [almost certainly Blauwen Molen] has disappeared from the landscape, being knocked to bits by high explosive'.

On the **23rd** 3/Hussars were based in Wytschaete, having been ready to move since 4 am, and remained in a state of readiness, but did not actually go up to the line until 4 pm – nothing much in itself, but it helps to indicate that time out of the line in the battle was often far from being relaxing. Again and again there are references to battalions being turned

The Indian Army has arrived – 129th Baluchis man defences in Wytschaete.

out, warned for the line and so on. In the line, digging trenches was far from easy for the cavalry – who were equipped neither with suitable tools nor, indeed, for the most part, with bayonets until later in the battle. This was hardly conducive to rest.

Further to the west on that day, 4/Hussars (minus eighty men and the machine guns in support) and 2/Munsters were relieved by 129th Baluchis. Commander Samson, with his 3 pdr gun mounted on a lorry and an armoured train, had been a feature of the defence of Hollebeke thus far. With the small gun on the lorry he 'was a remarkable shot', … 'but was somewhat of an embarrassment to us [4/Hussars] owing to his foible for wandering between the British and German lines'.

One of the problems of defending the Hollebeke position was the railway.

> *From the canal bend north of Hollebeke down to Kortewilde the railway was on a high embankment, fully exposed to the fire from both sides. It therefore became a matter of extreme difficulty to maintain touch between troops on either side of it, patrols being shot at as they approached.*

The men of 4/Hussars left behind in support made themselves very busy. Gathering up what civilian labour they could, they set about digging a second line along the north bank of the canal, to the north of Hollebeke, from the broken bridge (one of several pre war failed attempts to build a

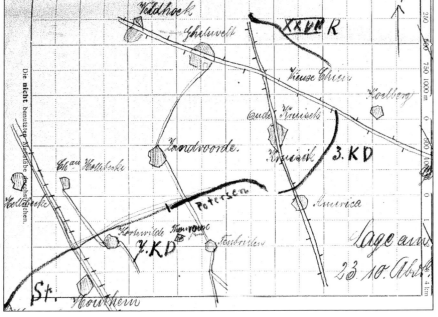

Situation Kruiseke - Zandvoorde - Hollebeke 23 Oct. 'Petersen' refers to a combined grouping of jäger battalions under the command of Major Petersen of Jäger Battalion 10.

crossing over the new Comines Canal) to the railway line. Over the next days, until 30 October, this work continued; and was to prove its worth in the fighting of that time.

The other area of concern for the cavalry was the position around Zandvoorde, which was held during these days by a rotation of 6 and 7 (Cavalry) Brigades; tentative probing advances were made by German cavalry and the positions – on a forward slope – periodically came under heavy fire. Casualties were suffered – for example, on 22 October 10/Hussars lost their CO (Colonel R Barnes DSO) and two other officers wounded and three ORs killed and ten wounded.

This rather unusual state of affairs, with quite heavy fighting going on north of the Menin Road and south of it a very bare defence that was subject to probing attacks but nothing more serious, was to continue for several more days.

On **25 October**, after forty eight hours' rest in farms around Kemmel, 11/Hussars came back into the line; the description gives some flavour of the life of the cavalry (and the infantry from the Indian Army) in the days leading up to 31 October.

Breakfasted at 3 am and reached Messines before daylight and at once took over the trenches east of the village from 9/Lancers. B and C went into the front trenches and A Squadron remained in support. The Regiment's line lay about a hundred yards in front of the village and joined up with the Connaught Rangers on the right ... and with the Bays on the left, the junction with the latter being effected on the Gapaard road, on which there was a barricade.

Messines had had a quiet time on the previous day and consequently some of the inhabitants, who had been absent for four days, returned from Wulverghem and Kemmel to feed their animals. The morning passed quietly except for some shells which fell near C Squadron who had exposed themselves while working on their trenches, which needed a good deal of improvement. The trenches occupied by B Squadron were better; they had been dug behind a bank and lean-to shelters had been made which gave some protection against shrapnel. The German trenches were some distance away and the German cavalry which occupied them seemed to be in good humour, as they kindly signalled back with a spade the results of shots fired at them by a few men of the Eleventh who had been detailed to fire at any German who showed himself. In the afternoon the German artillery came to life and subjected the village to a violent shelling, the convent [in fact the Institution Royale, a school for the daughters of Belgian army officers] *near the church coming in for particular attention. ...*

In the early morning 5/DG relieved the Regiment in the front line. As they left their quagmires and came into the village the men of the Eleventh presented a sorry sight, plastered in mud from head to foot. ... Colonel Pitman arranged for hot tea and fires to be ready in Messines for the men when they were relived. Two hours were spent in the battered houses, while they were getting warm and dry, and then the squadrons went into the support trenches half a mile to the west of Messines [in the area of Messines Military Cemetery today].

The British *OH*, quoting German sources, states that the German failure to remove the Cavalry Corps was because

... the British positions were too strong; that, as with the British, ammunition was beginning to fail; and that further attacks on Messines without heavy artillery was hopeless. The armament and equipment of the German cavalry was, it is admitted,

Messines Church on 25 October; the Institution Royale was on the right.

unsuitable for anything but mounted action. Incidentally, it is stated that British rifle and machine gun fire was so accurate that it was impossible to get within a thousand yards of the position.

Meanwhile, the allies were still working on the supposition of a general advance; French's orders for the 25th, repeated on the 26th, indicated that any British advance would be undertaken by keeping touch by the left; for it was the French, on the left of the line, who were to be the driving force of the offensive action.

29

On **26 October** the Cavalry Corps achieved very little. De Lisle's 1st Division and its supporting infantry from the Ferozepore Brigade – minus 2 Brigade, which had been sent south on the 25th to assist I Corps and therefore had lost half its cavalry strength – headed towards Oosttaverne and Garde Dieu but withdrew from any gains because of the situation on 7th Division's right flank and because the new line was inferior to the old – and would have required much work to make it secure. 11/Hussars was in Corps Reserve, centred on a farm (later known as Boyle's Farm) on the Wulverghem road, near the junction with a road to Kruisstraat Cabaret. 2nd Division's advance from Hollebeke was abandoned for similar reasons. 7th Division's problems resulted in elements of 7 (Cavalry) Brigade, then in reserve in Klein Zillebeke woods, moving to cover its withdrawal from the area and then the brigade took over the line from 6 (Cavalry) Brigade the next day.

1/Connaughts, as recorded by the regimental history, were fully occupied on the 26th. German shelling of Messines had become gradually more intense over the course of the preceding days, particularly on the 25th. At about noon on the 26th:

> *... they began shelling the church, apparently imagining that the tower was being used as a look-out post. 'There was nothing to be done,' says Fr Peal, 'to save the building. Most of our men were away in the firing line. The few that remained rushed in and carried away all that could be removed – statues, candles-sticks, pictures and rich vestments ... There was a large crucifix hanging by the sanctuary rails. Several efforts were made to remove it, but it was too firmly fixed. The men were very reluctant to leave it to the devouring flames and had to be ordered out. A day later, when everything was in ruins, pulpit, organ, altars, statues in stone, this crucifix remained untouched.'*

The battalion was relieved that afternoon:

> *Throughout the relief the enemy kept up shrapnel and rifle fire on the Rangers, causing casualties: one man killed (Private Hughes)* [though, curiously enough, he does not appear on the CWGC website] *and eighteen men wounded. Hughes was killed in leaving the trenches and, owing to the risk to other lives in bringing in the body, it had to be left till dark, when it was brought in on a door frame and buried in the garden of the still burning convent* [Institute/Institution Royal]. *Another Ranger (Private H Rogers –* [who is recorded by the CWGC]*) was buried besides Hughes two*

30

The ruined interior of Messines Church but with the crucifix undamaged.

days later and, as Fr Peal records, at the first respite in the firing comrades amongst the Rangers came and planted crosses over their graves.

However, they did not have much rest, as the battalion was order to attack the Gapaard trenches late that afternoon, in co-operation with the 57th and 2 Brigade. Already ground conditions that would become all too familiar as the war progressed were evident:

The ground in front of the Rangers to be traversed was open, with little cover, comprising a series of low elevations, gradually falling away towards the Germans near Gapaard.

The advance, setting off from south east of Wytschaete, was confused by the ground and the poor light conditions, not helped by a mist, and touch was never made with the 57th on the left. It seems that only part of C Company actually got in amongst the Germans:

It then, as it neared the enemy, came under a sharp fire. The men quickly closed on the German trenches, opened a heavy fire and rushed the trenches with the bayonet. They captured three trenches in succession, inflicting considerable losses on the enemy and taking an officer and two men prisoner.

An order had halted the advance at about 7 pm; meanwhile, C Company held on to its gains until midnight, exchanging sporadic fire with German outposts. It withdrew back to Wytschaete, reaching the village at about 3 am on the 27th. One man was killed and fifteen wounded, with one man missing, during the action.

For 3/Hussars, the 26th ended in 'a beastly wet night in the trenches'. Civilians were still in the front line trenches – for example, some of the officers of 3/Hussars were based in the convent: 'We gave the nuns some money for their poor people before we left and they were very pleased'. Some had meals in estaminets, 'in a very nice little pub [adjacent to the convent]. There was a funny old patron here, who each time the shelling started, got up a cart and began to load up his beer to be taken away. When it stopped back came the beer again.' Meanwhile, even in the trenches, 'occasional civilians approached but were not allowed through and were sent back'. On the 27th: 'An unfortunate little girl of some nine years of age was killed by a shell on the Wytschaete road'. Men in a barn on the same day had a close call when 'a couple of shells came through the roof of a barn in which a support troop were asleep, but not a man was touched'. On the 28th, in the evening, heading out on relief at about 6 pm, a German battery (located near Garde Dieu) opened up on the village, killing a nun and wounding other non-combatants. In Vierstraat,

All shelter was crowded with refugee Belgians, but a little cover was found for the men, who were well able to rest after ten days of strenuous life in the trenches. Ten days out of twelve continuously on the alert day in, day out.

Belgian refugees were both a sad sight and a considerable obstacle to troop movement.

The situation remained 'quiet' on the Cavalry Corps front for the next couple of days; although the instructions for an advance remained, these were dependent, as before, on movement on the left and there was very little of that. Higher command remained optimistic about the general situation, though reports from reconnaissance aircraft on the 28th indicated that there were masses of German transport on the roads between Roulers and Moorslede.

The care of horses took up considerable manpower in a cavalry regiment.

Chapter Two

30 October – 2 November
The Assault on Messines, Wytschaete, Hollebeke and Zandvoorde

In October 1914 a series of cavalry actions took place around the area of the Messines Ridge, but it was not until the German attempts to break through to the west from north of Ypres began to falter that the focus of operations shifted to this operationally significant area. In an attempt to inject momentum into the offensive, Supreme Army Headquarters took the decision to create the so-called 'Army Group Fabeck'. Commanded by General der Infanterie von Fabeck and with staff functions provided by Headquarters XIII Corps from Württemberg (Chief of Staff: Oberstleutnant von Loßberg, a man who was to become increasingly important as the war dragged on), the new grouping brought together XV Corps and II Bavarian Corps. Further reinforcement was provided by 26th Infantry Division, commanded by Generalleutnant Wilhelm Duke of Urach and Count of Württemberg, and the newly raised 6th Bavarian Reserve Division.

General der Infanterie von Fabeck.

The new formation was subordinated to Sixth Army, commanded by Generaloberst Crown Prince Rupprecht of Bavaria. Speed was of the essence so, with minimum delay, the force was moved into position along the rough line Deûlémont - Wervicq. Its orders were to relieve the light cavalry screening forces and then to drive forward in a northwesterly direction, aiming at a major breakthrough south of Ypres. General der Kavallerie Georg von der Marwitz, in command of all the cavalry in the area, described the overall plan in a letter to his wife dated 29 October.

Generalleutnant Duke Wilhelm of Urach, Commander 26th Infantry Division.

Generaloberst Crown Prince Rupprecht of Bavaria, Commander Sixth Army.

General der Kavallerie Georg von der Marwitz, pictured in Stettin in 1911 as Commander 3rd Infantry Division.

I believe that I can write to you about the forthcoming operations, because they begin early tomorrow morning. From the Menin – Ypres road, the enemy position bends away sharply southwest and west. From there to Messines my divisions are dug in facing the enemy. The total length of the frontage is about sixteen kilometres. The regiments have held on to these positions for about eight days now, whilst their horses have been held south of the Lys. Now today comes relief. Two and a half corps under Fabeck are to launch an assault on Ypres via Wervicq and Comines. Our men are going to be relieved in the line at about midnight then march back six to eight kilometres to the horses. Instead of them the infantry will be manning the trenches and then tomorrow and after an absolutely crazy bombardment on the enemy positions, everyone is going to attack with as much surprise as possible.

If the attack is successful, the enemy line will be pierced and their situation as far as the sea will be untenable. By the time my letter reaches you, you may already have read about a successful battle. It could well be decisive for the northern theatre of operations. I pray to God that he may grant our troops success! The assault may overrun the forward enemy positions with ease then the follow up thrust may develop extraordinary power and send them all packing. On the other hand it could easily stall in front of the front line and then again there may be other positions in rear of the first ones, so that the attack will have to be phased. Based on these thoughts, you should be able to determine from reports of Supreme Army Headquarters how things turned out at Ypres on 30 October.

In order to maximise the chances of success, speed was of the essence. Formations were quickly moved towards their starting positions and the commander and chief of staff spent all of 28 October on the road, making contact with all the various headquarters involved in the proposed operation and orientating themselves on the latest situation at the front. The overall Army Group Fabeck plan visualised an attack on the right flank by XV Corps with its axis of advance exclusive of the Ypres - Menin road and with its left flank following the line of the Comines -Ypres canal. This was also the flank where most of its heavy artillery, such as it was, was to be located. To the south and stretching away as far as Garde Dieu were the units and formations of II Bavarian Corps, which was to carry the main weight of the attack. Further left again was 26th Infantry Division, commanded by Generalleutnant Duke Wilhelm of Urach and Count of Württemberg. Fresh from the fighting near Fromelles, it was destined to play the leading role in the assault on and capture of Messines village and the surrounding area. In support of the planned renewed offensive and to extend the attack frontage further to the south a diversionary attack was launched against St Yves and Ploegsteert Wood by troops drawn from HKK (Senior Cavalry Commander) 1, and XIX Corps. In short, in conjunction with Fourth Army (Duke Albrecht of Württemberg) to its north and Sixth Army (Crown Prince Rupprecht) to its south, it was to force a breakthrough from the south west of Ypres. The operations were to begin on 29 October.

In fact the allies still planned an advance on 29 October – and, indeed on 30 October; which again failed to materialise. The main problem faced by the Cavalry Corps lay in the small scale tactical advances made by the troops opposite – small parties occupied farms or enclosures during the night and then fortified them and then continued the process the following evening. The Cavalry Corps lacked sufficient artillery to deal with this – Allenby was given old 6inch howitzers, but these were patently inadequate. French felt fairly optimistic about the situation, as did Joffre, the French commander in chief, the man who had provided most of the manpower for this proposed allied advance. Thus the events of 30 October came as a complete surprise and finally put paid to any idea of a general advance from Ypres: rather it was a matter of deploying troops to enable the position to be held.

Joseph Joffre.

Time constraints always influence military operations but for the German army, in this case, time for planning and preparation was so limited that the chances of success were severely compromised before battle had even been joined. One problem in particular was the fact that the various forces involved had no alternative but to spend all of 29 October manoeuvring into assembly areas; no sooner had this been achieved than the assaulting troops were involved in long drawn out marches through unfamiliar territory so as to be on the line of departure by dawn on 30 October.

As a result, the men of some units had been on their feet for over twenty four hours before H Hour, were almost exhausted and had been granted no time for reconnaissance or other orientation before the attacks began. As if that were not concern enough, it was clear from the outset that there was insufficient artillery to prepare and then support the advance properly.

Quite apart from the lack of sufficient heavy guns and the poor state of training of much of the field artillery, even the most stringent rationing of shells elsewhere along the Western Front did not yield enough ammunition to support this highly ambitious undertaking properly. Initially, such were the demands elsewhere that the only artillery, apart from the organic units of the formations involved, comprised part of 1st Battalion Guards Foot Artillery and 1st Battalion Foot Artillery Regiment 4 with heavy field howitzers. There were also a number of heavy howitzers from II Bavarian Corps and 1st Battalion Foot Artillery Regiment 14, together with heavy howitzers from half of 1st Battalion Foot Artillery Regiment 19 and one 300 mm howitzer battery from 26th Infantry Division. For some unexplained reason, four heavy howitzer batteries of 2nd Battalion Bavarian Reserve Foot Artillery Regiment 3 were kept in reserve.

Oberstleutnant Fritz von Loßberg, chief of staff to Headquarters

Army Group Fabeck, who had spent the previous twenty fours rushing around to familiarise himself with the situation and the ground, was all too aware of the scale of the problems the offensive would face.

We were convinced that the assault of Army Group Fabeck was going to bump up against stiff resistance because the time delay on this previously planned attack to the south of Ypres (the orders for which had only just been given), had provided the enemy time to move up reinforcements. Having strengthened their front along the lower Yser by flooding, they were then able to move the formations thus released south to counter Army Group Fabeck and the left flank of Fourth Army. [In addition] with the exception of 6th Bavarian Reserve Division, almost all the units of Army Group Fabeck had been severely reduced in strength as a result of previous battles and, above all, from the very first days of the battle, there was a serious lack of artillery ammunition, which became worse and worse with the onset of offensive operations, thus making reduction of stubbornly defended woods and strongly-built villages increasingly difficult.

Oberstleutnant Fritz von Loßberg, Chief of Staff Army Group Fabeck pictured later as a generalmajor.

In view of all these difficulties, General von Fabeck requested a postponement of twenty four hours; but the request was turned down out of hand by Supreme Army Command. The attack was to go ahead on 30 October as planned and would be supported by Fourth Army to the north and Sixth Army on the southern flank. All discussion over, the die was cast. XV Corps, attacking with 30th Infantry Division right and 39th Infantry Division left, was to take over the frontage formerly held by the cavalry of Marwitz and was to attack between the Menin-Ypres road

General der Kavallerie Georg von der Marwitz, Commander of all German cavalry south of Ypres, October 1914.

and the Ypres-Comines canal, with the aim of breaking through to Ypres, before pushing on further west. Just prior to the attack, the Corps Commander issued a special order of the day which, strangely, made mention of Canadian forces, who in fact would not arrive in the Salient for another five months.

> *Tomorrow, in conjunction with Bavarian II Corps and 26th Infantry Division, we are to attack the British around Zandvoorde and to the east of that place and then push on to Ypres. This breakthrough is of decisive importance for the outcome of the war. Therefore we shall and must be victorious! His Majesty the Kaiser trusts that each will try his utmost to do his duty. We shall make sure that we justify this trust. Brave and undaunted, we are going to attack the British, Indians,*

Situation Army Group Fabeck 30 October.

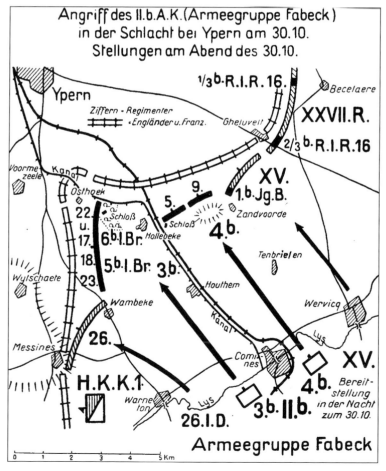

Canadians, Moroccans and all such rabble. The enemy is becoming worn out and recently, whenever we have gone for them energetically, they have surrendered in large numbers. So let us go forward with God for our Kaiser and our beloved German Fatherland!

II Bavarian Army Corps, whose sector was designated the *Schwerpunkt* [point of main effort], was unable to issue its orders until the afternoon of 29 October - a clear demonstration of how compressed the timeframe for preparation of the attack was.

1. General von Fabeck intends to deploy the Bavarian II Army Corps to break through the enemy positions along the line of the canal. To our right, XV Corps will also go on the offensive and 26th Infantry Division will attack to our left. Strong forces echeloned in depth behind the inner flanks of these neighbouring

A battered Chateau Hollebeke.

formations are in place to prevent Bavarian II Army Corps from being vulnerable to outflanking manoeuvres after it has broken through. A general reserve will be formed from 6th Bavarian Reserve Division and one heavy howitzer battalion.

2. The Schwerpunkt [point of main effort] *of the attack is placed on the inner flank of the two divisions and is directed at the village and chateau of Hollebeke. So, once the canal has been crossed, permanent contact is to be maintained between the two divisions. Having gained the heights northwest of Baskerville and the Rozebeek sector, the next strong points to the rear are to be assaulted immediately and preferably with fresh troops.*

3. The attack will begin at daybreak 30 October when, without further order, the artillery is to range in. As soon as this is complete and the artillery is ready to start its bombardment, the infantry is to begin immediately to advance so as to force the enemy to man its positions. The artillery is to bring down effective fire against the occupied positions. Harassing fire simply squanders ammunition and is forbidden. Every effort is to be made to profit from the flanking effect of interdivisional cross fire. Artillery operating from the 4th Division sector is to superimpose its fire on the Zandvoorde area.

4. A field gun battery is to be allocated in direct support of each of the infantry regiments in the front line. When this happens they are removed from the command of their parent artillery formations.

5. By 6.00 pm 29 October at the latest, Commander 4 Field Artillery Brigade (less his staff) is to report to the Corps command post in Comines and act as artillery adviser until further notice. Placed at his disposal are Oberstleutnant Gramich and Hauptmann Lehmann from Corps Headquarters, one orderly officer from each of 3 Field Artillery Brigade and Foot Artillery Regiment Gartmeyer and six despatch riders from the cavalry of each division.

Operating on the right flank of XV Corps, 39th Infantry Division split its sector into three sub-sectors. On the right and attacking on a narrow front, Infantry Regiment 132 was tasked with the capture of Zandvoorde Chateau, 700 metres east of Zandvoorde. On the left, 82 Infantry Brigade, less one battalion, was made responsible for the central and western sections of Zandvoorde. In between these two groupings was inserted a composite force of four jäger battalions from HKK [Senior Cavalry

Commander] 2 under Major Petersen, commanding officer Jäger Battalion 10.

From the British perspective the next fortnight or so becomes increasingly confusing as regards the order of battle; battalions – and parts of battalions, brigades and even divisions (for example, 3rd (Cavalry) Division went from Allenby's command to Haig's for a while, having only recently been under Rawlinson's) were shifted according to the requirements of the rapidly changing situation. As the intense fighting developed, further possibilities for misunderstandings in command and control arose with the arrival of significant numbers of French troops and, to a lesser extent, of Indian Army units intermingled with British troops along the narrow frontage.

It is an unfortunate side of much military history writing that the unglamorous side of war – logistics above all – tends to get neglected when factoring in the difficulties of conducting fighting operations. The problems of communications and supply need emphasising – something, of course, that applied to all armies. It was, as the *OH* comments,

> *... practically impossible to pass messages along or parallel to the front as the troops were in lengths of trench separated by considerable distances. Information, ... owing to the special liability of damage to wires parallel to the front, had to be sent back to division and corps headquarters, whence it was distributed forward again. This system required a considerable quantity of wire which was often cut. Generally speaking, during the Battles of Ypres, telephone equipment of all kinds was very scarce and the lines bad; messages forwarded by divisional headquarters were almost exclusively sent by runners.*

Supplying the BEF was almost equally difficult. The main port during the retreat of the BEF was at St Nazaire; on 13 October Le Havre took its place and Rouen was also reopened on 13 October. Boulogne was used as a subsidiary base, mainly for ammunition and wounded, from the same date. Of course, from these ports everything had to be moved to the front and this was a demanding matter of how to use the limited railway network, especially when the French armies also needed to be supplied, often on the same lines. Once at the railhead – the various ones, such as Steenbecque, Hazebrouck etc, assigned to particular formations – supplies had to be moved to 'refilling' points. There was little or no co-ordination by the allies on the use of roads and the French (the British complained) did not consult or inform. Transports could meet on roads that were paved only for the width of one vehicle and, with very muddy ground on either side, chaos often ensued, with delays the inevitable consequence. Finally, the British sent staff officers to manage difficult crossing places and imposed order, regardless of the laid down routes.

30th October

The principal German assault was launched from south east of Ypres and along the Menin Road.

Haig, whose I Corps now had three divisions – the 1st, 2nd and 7th – had ordered his commanders to dig in on the best possible positions where they held the line and to engage in active reconnaissance, despite the fact that an advance had been ordered for the following day. It was a sensible move, which proved its worth in the days to come. Haig's front ran for seven and a half

Douglas Haig.

miles. Allenby, headquartered in Kemmel, had an even greater problem to face; his Corps had a line of some nine miles to defend, from the Douve to Zandvoorde, with his three cavalry divisions and two attached Indian Army battalions – the 57th and 129th. Including supports and reserves, this gave him about a thousand rifles per mile to cover this frontage, whilst his artillery consisted almost entirely of Royal Horse Artillery, equipped with relatively light 13 pounders. Allenby did manage to create a Corps reserve, three regiments from each of 2nd (Cavalry) Division's brigades and an RHA battery and positioned it at Klein Zillebeke under the command of the CO of the Scots Greys, Bulkeley-Johnson.

In essence the Germans intended to launch an attack along the whole of the Ypres front, but by far the main effort was to be carried out by Army Group Fabeck; the initial objective was to be the capture of Zandvoorde and the clearing of Messines Ridge. From there the heights around Kemmel would be taken, with the result that allied troops to the north and in front of Ypres would be cut off and pushed back to the sea.

Zandvoorde

As soon as it was sufficiently light on the morning of 30 October for German artillery observers to be able to correct fire, several batteries fired three salvoes to indicate the start of the bombardment of the British positions. On this occasion at least, the fire plan was heavy and reasonably effective. After the known locations had been softened up for an hour, the attack was launched all along the Army Group frontage. Wherever possible attacks were extremely concentrated; that of Infantry

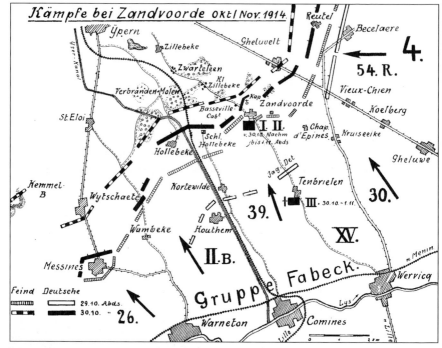

The assault on Zandvoorde from 30 October; note the rather optimistic 'capture' of Messines on 30 October.

Regiment 132, for example, was an assault with two battalions in the front line, each on a 350 metre frontage. Visibility was in fact so poor that morning that it was 8.00 am before the guns opened fire and 9.00 am before these two battalions, each reinforced by an engineer platoon to deal with obstacles and a machine gun platoon, launched their attacks, each with two companies forward.

Although the battlefield was basically flat, with extensive fields of fire in places, there were, in fact, numerous obstacles to movement. Everywhere there were hedges, copses and dense woods, whilst the ubiquitous Flanders drainage ditches of varying depth and width ran in all directions. In addition to these physical problems, the advancing troops came under heavy small arms fire almost as soon as they crossed their start lines and enemy artillery fire fell amongst them constantly. Despite these issues, reasonable progress was made and 3rd Battalion Infantry Regiment 132, in reserve, pushed forward towards 2nd Battalion, with the regimental band in close attendance. By late morning the 1st Battalion was already fighting through the depth of the British

44

positions in places but, out to the right, the attackers had been checked by the moat of Zandvoorde Chateau (see Map 8, p.50 – Zandvoorde 'Chateau' was in fact a large farm) and the obstinate defence being put up by 1st Royal Welsh Fusiliers. The pressure was maintained, however, and the chateau, which was the main divisional objective for that day, was captured reasonably quickly.

On the 2nd Battalion front, the presence of dense woodland and near-impenetrable thickets made progress and the maintenance of momentum extremely difficult. However, even here, once the chateau was in German hands matters became easier. Here the defence was mainly the responsibility of the dismounted elements of the British 7th Cavalry Brigade and there were simply too few of them to be able to withstand an infantry assault pushed forward aggressively and in strength. Of course the attackers did not have it all their own way. The regimental commander, Oberst Kreyenberg, deployed his 3rd Battalion forward later in the day and had the regimental band play suitable

A captured British fire trench in Zandvoorde, connected to the building behind by a 'mousehole'. (Lambrecht Collection)

45

martial music to encourage his men but eventually many hours of bitter fighting died away with the men of Infantry Regiment 132 holding on precariously to extremely exposed positions between Zandvoorde Chateau and the actual oratory at Chapelle d'Epines. In order to force a way forward, a pair of guns from 2nd Battery Field Artillery Regiment 66 were moved into locations from which direct fire could be brought down against the enemy positions from very close range. Once this fire See map p. 50 became effective, the attack was resumed and pressed home, though at high cost, especially amongst the junior leadership, a number of whom fell whilst spearheading the assault so as to provide a good example to their men. By the end of the day all the objectives were taken and numerous men from the Royal Welch Fusiliers and the South Staffs were captured.

For the British defenders, the attack commenced with heavy shelling from 6.45 am on trenches held by 7 (Cavalry) Brigade's 1st and 2nd Life Guards, about 400 men. The trenches were narrow, on a forward slope – therefore clearly visible to the enemy – and with only minimal head cover. Inevitably, the defenders would be shelled out of them and the support line was manned. The infantry assault came at 8 am; the defending troops (along with the Royal Horse Guards (RHG) machine guns) were overrun. Very few of them made it back to the British lines and, indeed, very few have identified graves.

Mobilisation of The Life Guards and Lieutenant Hon WM Wyndham.

The 1st and 2nd Life Guards were largely composed of reservists – certainly in the case of 1/Life Guards. RA Lloyd, in his excellent memoir, *A Trooper in the Tin Hats*, related what happened soon after the outbreak of war:

> *A Composite Regiment of Household Cavalry was formed at once, each regiment contributing one service squadron of four sixteen-file troops. In addition, our regiment provided the Headquarters of the Composite Regiment. This effort pretty well cleared out the whole of the regiment.*

To make up numbers, reservists were called up and also a King's Pardon was issued for those who had deserted; the new commanding officer was the Duke of Teck. Amongst the officers from the reserve and who climbed back into uniform was William Reginald Wyndham, who had managed to wangle a posting to 1/Life Guards, even though his original regiment was 17/Lancers. His arrival at Knightsbridge Barracks caused a small sensation, according to Lloyd; he was:

Dressed in a rig-out which was a sight for the gods. His khaki jacket fitted him where it touched him; his riding pants were of coarse material, baggy and reminiscent of knickerbockers at the knees. He wore in addition a pair of thick greased hob-nailed ankle boots, rough puttees, and a cap from which the wire had been removed and which looked as if it had been slept on. On his Sam Browne belt was a stout iron hook from which dangled a pair of hedging-and-ditching gloves. Before he had advanced ten paces inside the barrack gate he was unanimously christened 'Sinbad the Sailor'. The nickname seemed to jump to the minds of all those who saw him and Sinbad he remained. In spite of his weird uniform, Sinbad was a fine soldier and a fine gentleman. When somebody chipped him about his turnout, I heard him reply in the deep, deliberate voice with which we were soon to be familiar: 'My dear sir, you will all be dressed like this, or worse, before Christmas'. He was right.

Lieutenant Wyndham was killed near Zwarteleen on 6 November; Lloyd commented:

So well liked was Sinbad among the troops that when darkness fell the same night two drivers from the machine gun section, Rubber Rivers and Tinker Underwood, got two horses and a half-limber, galloped up to the scene of the counter attack and brought back his body for burial in the nearby churchyard [Zillebeke, where he lies today].

1/Life Guards had C Squadron and two troops of D in the trenches on the night of 29 October. The War Diary reported on the events of the 30th:

6 am: Heavy bombardment of position opened. At 7.30 am position was attacked by large force of infantry. This attack proved successful owing to greatly superior numbers. Regiment retired in good order about 10 am except C Squadron on left flank from which only about ten men got back. Remainder of squadron missing. Also one machine gun put out of action.

Regiment retired behind 6th Brigade, which turned out to support. 2nd Dragoons and 3rd and 4th Hussars also came to support, but did not come into action. Having gained Zandvoorde Ridge enemy did not press the attack very vigorously, and second position occupied by 6 Brigade was not attacked.

Besides listing eight or so killed or wounded, the diary noted that Captains Lord Hugh Grosvenor and E Kelly and Lieutenants Ward and Close-Brooks were missing – in fact all killed and commemorated on the Menin Gate, along with a hundred rank and file, of whom few are listed as killed on this day by the CWGC.

Lloyd was with the horse lines that morning, with about sixty others, in a small wood on the edge of Verbrandenmolen:

There was no tendency on our part to oversleep on the morning of 30 October. Round about our ears six hundred cold, hungry horses were splashing in the mud, and the morning was frosty and raw. We were up and about with the first streak of dawn, and spent a hectic half hour trying to water and feed the poor brutes. Before we had quite got through this operation a hellish bombardment broke out upon Zandvoorde Ridge. It was the hottest we had heard up to then. One idea formed itself immediately in all our minds – this was the expected big German attack. We felt, too, it was right on the little patch of front held by our own people. For upwards of an hour the ground trembled and the air was full of din. Then gradually the shelling subsided and the machine gun and rifle fire swelled up into a roar. We finished feeding the horses, then rallied round the cooks' fire and snatched whatever was going for breakfast.

Gradually, about 8.30 or 9 am, the rifle fire grew less lively. It is amazing how rumour travels at such moments of crisis. It was soon being whispered in detached groups round the various fires that the line had been broken and that the regiment had suffered heavily.

Lloyd shortly afterwards got hold of a horse and went up towards the ridge. He met

Hubert Bussey with his forehead cut open and bleeding. He was walking calmly back, smoking a cigarette and looking for the dressing station. Obviously he was badly shaken. I could get no information from him. ... Round the next bend I met Gus Russell. He was limping along carrying a machine gun tripod. His machine gun had been hit and put out of action ... In the midst of this havoc the Germans came over in masses and by sheer weight of numbers had gained a footing in our trenches, which had been almost obliterated by shelling... At dusk the survivors hobbled back to the horse lines on being relieved by the Foot Guards. They looked bedraggled and weary to death as they marched in. Sinbad the Sailor [Wyndham], covered in mud, and with a rifle slung over his shoulder like a Tommy, walked alone at the head of what remained of his Troop.

This, of course, impacted on the neighbouring 7th Division. At first it was not clear what was going on – the news of the loss of the village got back to I Corps at 8.30 am and then had to be forwarded to 7th Division and, in turn, to 22 Brigade headquarters, closest to Zandvoorde, and to 21 Brigade nearby. From about 10 am the battalions that held the line from the village to Kruiseecke – from west to east, 1/Royal Welsh Fusiliers (RWF), 2/Royal Scots Fusiliers (RSF) and 2/Green Howards (GH), were thus exposed to flanking fire from rifles and the German artillery that was brought up to the newly captured and dominating ground.

The support line was to the west of the village, in low lying ground. Byng ordered 6 Brigade to send two regiments forward from Klein Zillebeke to cover the retreat whilst at the same time preparing a position in front of Klein Zillebeke, rather more secure from artillery fire as it was on low ground amongst trees. 22 Brigade's commander (Brigadier General Lawford) ordered his reserve battalions to cover the retreat of 7 (Cavalry) Brigade as well and possibly recapture Zandvoorde.

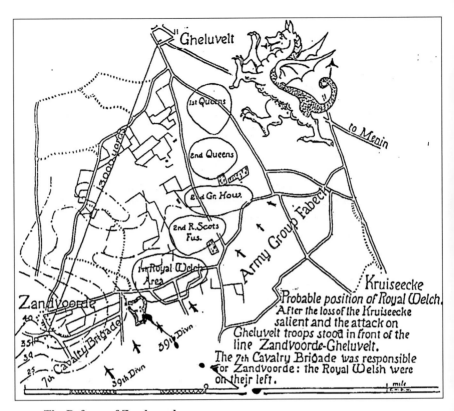

The following are labels visible within the map:

Gheluvelt

1st Queens

2nd Queens

2nd Gr. How.

2nd R.Scots Fus.

1st Royal Welch Area

Zandvoorde

to Menin

Army Group Fabeck

Kruiseecke

1300 contour

6 Cavalry Brigade

39th Divn

35th
34
25
7th Cav.
39th Divn

Probable position of Royal Welch. After the loss of the Kruiseecke salient and the attack on Gheluvelt troops stood in front of the line Zandvoorde-Gheluvelt. The 7th Cavalry Brigade was responsible for Zandvoorde: the Royal Welsh were on their left.

1 mile

The Defence of Zandvoorde.

Bulkeley Johnson's force, at Haig's request, was used to harden 6 (Cavalry) Brigade's line between Hollebeke and Zandvoorde and to join in any attempt to recapture the latter village. At 9.15 am Haig sent Major General Bulfin (newly promoted, on 26 October) with the two battalions of I Corps' reserve to a point between Veldhoek and Zandvoorde with the same intention of assisting in restoring the line at Zandvoorde.

Major W Willcox, 3/Hussars, on arrival with his regiment at Klein Zillebeke, was detailed off on attachment to Bulkeley Johnson, getting there about 11.00 am.

I ... immediately had to take a message to Sir Douglas Haig at the I Corps Headquarters about a mile east of Ypres [ie the White Chateau – one of many so called during the war] *and inform him of the arrival of the three regiments* [of Bulkeley Johnson's force]. *As I rode up to the chateau the general was pacing up and down the verandah, and I saw the most undisturbed looking general of*

50

all the generals I had seen during the last few days… 'Here's word from the cavalry,' he said, as I walked up the steps, 'Go in and tell Gough [ie Brigadier General J Gough VC, Haig's chief of staff]' *and pointing to the door.*

All of this had become somewhat academic for 1/RWF; in an exposed position, they could only retire over open ground and the Germans had already taken up a position to their right rear. The casualties were horrendous; the CO, Lieutenant Colonel H Cadogan, was killed (his body was later recovered and he is amongst the few of the battalion's dead that day who has a named grave, in Hooge Crater Cemetery) along with nine officer and 320 OR casualties. Eight six men answered the evening roll call and the sad remnant of the battalion was attached for some days afterwards to 2/Queen's. For them, by midday it was all over. The two battalions on its left managed to fend off the German enveloping movement from their right and a new line was eventually secured, 1,200 yards in the rear, by the arrival of the reinforcing troops.

The RWF history tried to sort out a complex story:

Our 1st Battalion, little over 400 strong, was scattered about in short slits of trenches, without inter-communication, on the forward slope of a roll in the plain; their field of vision was short in the midst of the hedge-enclosed fields, and it was impossible to know what was happening to the right or left. But the advancing lines of German infantry were mowed down by their rifle fire.

However, the situation on the right was disastrous, as the Household Cavalry had been forced out of their positions on the Zandvoorde ridge but no news of this reached the RWF – or Brigadier General Lawford. The first inkling that the men of 22 Brigade had of the seriousness of the situation was when German artillery opened up in enfilade from Zandvoorde. Thus, under frontal attack, under enfilade fire, and now increasingly being taken in the rear as Germans moved behind the position from the newly captured ground around Zandvoorde, the flanking posts of 1/RWF were inexorably being overrun. To 1/RWF's left, the Scots Fusiliers and Green Howards managed to extricate themselves to the new line.

Lieutenant E Wodehouse of 1/RWF – wounded and fated to spend the war as a prisoner or interned – described what happened:

We were holding a line about three-quarters of a mile long …

Battalion HQ was in a dugout about six hundred yards to the rear. The trenches were not well sited for field of fire. So far as I know, no one was on our right; some 'Blues' [RHG] were supposed to be there, but I did not see them. It was foggy in the early morning, so that the Germans could not shell us much, which was lucky, as they had two batteries on Zandvoorde Ridge. About 8 am the shelling increased and we saw large numbers of German soldiers advancing down a slope about 1,500 yards to our front. Also I believe large numbers were seen coming round our exposed right flank. The batteries on the ridge were now firing point blank into our trenches, so that it was difficult to see what was happening, and the rifle fire also increased from our right rear. No orders were received, so it was thought best to stay where we were, and about midday the whole battalion was either killed, wounded or taken prisoners. ... [After he was taken prisoner he observed that] the Germans were suffering heavily from our shell fire and were unable to use the road. I saw some of their guns get stuck in the mud behind the village.

The new line in rear that was established ran from Hollebeke Chateau; a squadron of RDGs there, followed by two of Bulkeley Johnston's force, 6 and 7 (Cavalry) Brigades, 2/Gordons, 1 S/Staffs, 2/Warwicks and 2/Bedfords; the latter was positioned just to the north of Zandvoorde and, beyond a gap, the hastily created refused flank of 2/RSF.

See map p. 55 The position of the Green Howards and the Scots Fusiliers was considered untenable; so in the early afternoon, under divisional orders, the Scots Fusiliers withdrew to conform to the new line which ran up to Gheluvelt and make contact with 3 Brigade in front that village. As a consequence of the fighting on the 30th and the 31st, 2/RSF, which only had about 400 men all told when the fighting began on the morning of the 30th, was reduced to two officers and some thirty men. The Green Howards, however, did not receive the orders until well on into the day – at 3.30 pm. Despite the nature of the ground across which they had to move during their withdrawal, it was achieved with the loss of only ten men (compared to 2/RSF's hundred in the same operation) – though the battalion was by then reduced to about 300 men. The CO, Lieutenant Colonel E King, was shot and killed by a sniper, one of seventy killed, excluding those who succumbed to wounds on subsequent days. Major Willcox again:

By midday a very severe struggle was raging between Zandvoorde and Klein Zillebeke, but for the rest of the day the cavalry held the German infantry who, in spite of the awful

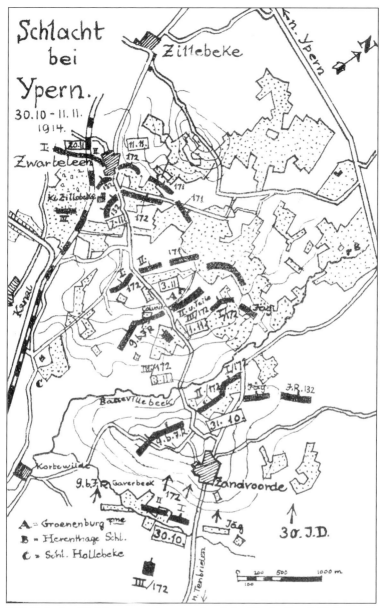

39th Infantry Division operations south of the Menin Road 30 Oct - 11 November.

shelling which supported them, could make no headway against us. The German shelling was tremendous; their 'Black Marias' were falling as far back as Zillebeke, while Klein Zillebeke and

its inn, which was the headquarters of the cavalry brigades, was
a tornado of bursting shells, and many casualties occurred there.
It was a most interesting spot, that inn. To it came Allenby, Byng
and staff officers of the Army and I Corps and behind it on the
railway line an armoured car – sailors, they said, but I don't
know, popping off a smallish gun gallantly but one imagines most
ineffectually against the masses of German howitzers. A dressing
station had been formed near the inn, and to it streamed, or were
carried, a continuous flow of wounded, while not two hundred
yards from the pub someone had reverently covered the appalling
remains of a motor cyclist despatch rider, who had met a German
shell, with a sack.

The Bedfords tried to advance against the Germans at 2 pm, to no avail. Instead, Bulfin had to release men from his detachment – 2/Sussex and 1/Northants – to support the troops in the line. Artillery had been brought forward, had been effective but had also suffered heavy casualties and had a number of guns disabled by German fire.

To the south, 3 (Cavalry) Brigade came under heavy shell fire at about noon; blown out of their trenches, they moved clear of Hollebeke but the road bridge over the Comines Canal was held. This left the chateau, on the east side of the canal, very vulnerable and, at about 2.30 pm, the squadron defending it abandoned its defence, but in good order.

Haig ordered, at about 12.30 pm, that the line from the bend in the canal at Hollebeke to the front of Gheluvelt should be held at all costs. He wanted to recreate the reserve behind Gheluvelt (2 Brigade), which could only be done once the new line had been established and stabilised and the brigade's two absent battalions, 1/Northants and 2/Sussex, returned. In fact this was all wishful thinking; what had been left of 2 Brigade had already been largely committed. Rather than withdrawing troops from the line, in fact a considerable part of 2nd Division's reserve – then west of Polygon Wood – was sent up. His line in the south was still in a far from satisfactory state, lacking any reserves and still very thinly spread. By the evening 2/Grenadiers and the Irish Guards had replaced 6 and 7 (Cavalry) Brigades in the line and 2/Ox & Bucks, late on, sent a couple of companies to replace the Engineers (23 Field Company) who had been thrown into the line early in the day. The fact that Engineers were being used at all as infantry is a clear indicator of the dire straits into which the British defence had been pressed.

 While all these British manoeuvres were occurring, towards mid afternoon the German 39th Infantry Division gave orders for a fresh thrust in the direction of Zillebeke. This would have required Infantry

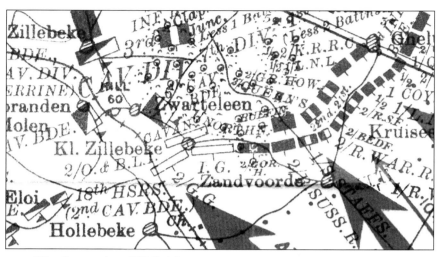

Situation evening of 30 October.

Regiment 132 to push on a further 800 metres beyond Zandvoorde, but it was simply beyond them physically. Worn out and weakened by the numerous casualties they had suffered, it proved to be impossible to reorganise the tangled sub units or to prepare them for another major effort. Despite all the pressure exerted by Generalleutnant von Kathen down the chain of command, he finally had to accept that there was no alternative but to direct that the troops in contact were to dig in along the line they had reached and prepare to defend against British counter-attacks.

Off to the north, Infantry Regiment 136 from 30th Infantry Division had moved into its assault position the previous night. It was flanked by Infantry Regiment 99 on its right and the right flank regiment of 39th Infantry Division on its left. Each regiment planned to attack with only three companies in the front line and the remainder echeloned back in depth. Promptly, just as planned, the artillery began to

Generalmajor von Lewinsky, Commander Field Artillery Regiment 80.

bombard enemy positions at 8.15 am. Then, an hour later, the order for the assault reached the forward brigade headquarters. Slowly, but surely and benefiting from effective fire support, the attack began to develop satisfactorily. During an advance of approximately 600 metres, Infantry Regiment 136 overran a number of minor enemy positions and several farm buildings. All this came at a price, however. The British defenders fought back vigorously, causing many casualties. Major Borck, commanding 2nd Battalion Infantry Regiment 136, was killed leading his men into action, as were Leutnants Schumann and Brinkmann. After about three hours of continuous fighting, Infantry Regiment 136 had advanced to the area of Chapelle d'Epines, i.e. about one and a half kilometres east of Zandvoorde. Infantry Regiment 99, on the other hand, had lost a large number of men, victims of flanking fire from the direction of Gheluvelt and found it so difficult to get forward that the entire assault in this sector was at risk of failing. This was clearly unacceptable and orders came directing Infantry Regiment 99 to advance towards Gheluvelt 'at all costs' (that depressing phrase which featured so frequently in directives issued by both sides during the battle). Shortly before 4.00 pm, Headquarters 30th Division reinforced this order, directing that the advance was to be continued until the line Zandvoorde – Gheluvelt was reached.

So much for the desirable. In the event the defenders, fighting from hastily constructed slit trenches, natural cover and reinforced buildings, put up strong resistance. Eventually, after a battle lasting for hours and at high cost, Infantry Regiment 136 managed to reach the line, but this success was not matched by its neighbours to the left and right. As a result, its flanking companies had to bend back their line, giving up ground previously won, in order to conform and to leave no gaps. Schütze Meister, a gunner with the machine gun company, later wrote an account which provides a flavour of the action that day.

On the morning of 30 October 1914 there was to be an attack right across the front. That morning the storm broke punctually. The first trench was taken with few casualties and we captured between 600 and 700 prisoners. We then pressed on. As we advanced in bounds, we saw a white flag being waved above the enemy trench, so we stood up and advanced on the enemy. However, it was a trick. Just as we approached to within one hundred metres, we were engaged from there with rifle and machine gun fire. As though an order had been given, we all hit the ground and then we continued forward in rushes, but there were heavy casualties. The second trench was captured and we

56

laid about us with rifle butts. Because the infantry was so tied up, Vizefeldwebel Mehlbräuer pushed on ahead with his platoon. We arrived at a farm which offered cover and he directed that the guns were to be placed in firing positions. He then went on ahead alone out of the farm, probably with the intention of placing a machine gun up on the hill, but the hill was occupied by the enemy. Vizefeldwebel Mehlbräuer did not get very far before we saw him hit and collapse. At that Unteroffizier Berning, who had assumed command of the platoon, gave orders that the guns were to go into action.

Unteroffizier Knauth, who served with 6th Company Infantry Regiment 136, described in detail the events which followed this hard day of battle. His is a typical and evocative account of the intense, exhausting fighting in the close country southwest of Ypres as November opened.

That night there was a strange, eerie silence. Hardly a single shot was heard and not a word was spoken aloud. A farmhouse

Men of Infantry Regiment 136 marching through Zandvoorde.

to our front was burning and lighting up the trees behind in a marvellous manner. It was not possible to distinguish flames, smoke and sparks, just the glow of the fire, sometimes brighter, sometimes fainter, which showed that a blaze was still burning there behind the walls. There was no crackling to be heard or falling beams to be seen, it was all rather like a theatrical backcloth, with one pointed gable end standing up like a church spire above the remaining blackened walls with their empty window sockets. As dawn broke the flames died out and only a few sad remains of walls stuck up into the sky.

Emerging like a shadowy figure out of the darkness our company feldwebel appeared and whispered to me, 'One volunteer per section is to go forward on listening duty.' Slowly and silently the thin file of men wrapped in their greatcoats disappeared. Within seconds, they had been swallowed by the darkness of the night. Gradually the clouds cleared and the stars emerged. For a great many of us this was the very last time that they would ever be able to look up at the endless starry heaven in all its beauty. At 6.00 am, still under the protection of darkness, a figure came up to our company feldwebel. They spoke together for a short time, then the figure disappeared once more. This was followed by a lively discussion amongst the platoon commanders down in the dugout. Soon all was quiet once more. A short while later my platoon commander arrived.

Has the attack been ordered?' I asked. 'Yes. The artillery opens up at 6.00 am to prepare the enemy positions for the assault.' That meant a stay of execution of another hour. Gradually it became light and I looked at my watch. Five minutes to go; then, passed on from mouth to mouth came the order, 'Fix bayonets! Make ready!' With a metallic clattering noise the bayonets were fixed. Would I be thrusting with my bayonet once more or not? If I did it would certainly be streaked with blood. A strange feeling came over me. It was not fear; that emerges only when we feel ourselves to be defenceless. But today we would be setting off calmly and sure of victory. If anyone was to fall, he would be falling in battle as a brave soldier, happily carrying out his duty to his Fatherland; as a victor, for not a man doubted that our operation would bring victorious success.

At exactly 6.00 am there was a dreadful rushing, roaring and groaning sound in the air, just as though all hell had broken loose Our artillery had opened fire. To our front the ground dropped away to the road, then rose gently once more. Our *artillery engaged the area on the far side of the road. Wherever the eye could see, smoke and pillars of earth were being thrown up by exploding shells with, between them, the small yellow clouds showing where shrapnel had burst. A road in the distance, lined with poplars, was brought under heavy fire and very soon a dozen snapped off tree trunks were lying in the road. Only a few hundred metres to our front rounds from a complete heavy battery were landing. It was a gruesomely fine sight. Our 210 mm howitzers were firing rapidly and all the smaller calibre guns, down to the lightest field guns, were contributing to the concert.*

There was almost no sound from the British artillery. On one occasion something whistled over our heads and impacted about two metres away in the soft ground, but the shell did not explode. Rapid small arms fire was then aimed at the British. Now and then the odd individual could be seen, but the enemy also fired back vigorously. One man leapt up out of the trench to take an order to the supporting platoon, but hardly had he broken cover than he gave a shout and fell, groaning terribly. A bullet had hit him in the abdomen. At the risk of their own lives, two men of the supporting platoon dragged him to safety. Shells whistled past, unpleasantly close to our heads, then we saw German infantry emerge from the wood to our left and begin to advance. It could not be long before it was our turn. Our comrades down below us did not seem to be under fire, then one suddenly fell, followed by another. They began to run forward and another one went down. The remainder disappeared behind the house that had been burning the previous night. A battalion runner appeared. '6th Company: attack!' he shouted, then disappeared once more. All of a sudden another runner appeared and bawled, '2nd Battalion: attack!' At that our company commander shouted. 'Right, with God's help, let's go!' Reserve Leutnant Knapmann was the first to plunge into the hail of bullets. Followed by my section, I climbed out of the trench as fast as possible and we ran as fast as we could after our Leutnant.

At first it appeared as though the British had been taken completely by surprise by our attack but no sooner had the other companies appeared than their bullets were whistling most unpleasantly around our ears. We ran as far as the road, but our way on the other side was blocked by a hedge. I ran up to it but, unfortunately, a few strands of wire ran through its twigs. Our company had now taken up a firing line with its front at ninety degrees to the road. To our right neighbouring troops had closed up to the thick hedge, which surrounded the farm to the right of the road. The British there seemed to be firing especially accurately, judging by the fall of shot, which was right in amongst the line.

Offizierstellvertreter Räbisch ordered, '6th Company! On your feet! Double march!' We took cover again just in front of the house. During the dash forward Räbisch had been grazed on the thigh by a bullet, but he took no notice. Drawing his sword and taking his pistol in his right hand, he entered the house to see if any of the enemy had hidden themselves there. Hardly had Räbisch entered the second room than he gave a groan and collapsed, with blood oozing out from beneath his helmet. Because I could see that simultaneously spurts of chalk were being thrown out of the wall on our side, I assumed that Räbisch had been hit by a German bullet but, by chance, I looked out of the window and saw where the shot had come from. Barely one hundred metres behind the house there was an enemy trench, in which the British were running up and down in some excitement.

In order to be able to maintain the link to 7th Company more easily, Leutnant Knapmann, I and a few other men rushed over the road into the ruins of the second house. The situation here was more or less the same as the other side, but this time there were no window openings in the direction of the enemy. At this point our howitzers opened fire on the trench to our front in order to help us get forward. We watched with uncontrolled joy as we saw how accurately our artillery was landing shells, this time directly on the trench. Not even the toughest British skulls could withstand that for long. Four times in succession there was a roaring sound just over us, so low that we feared the shells would collapse our gable end, but then there were four dreadful explosions one hundred metres to our front, so strong that they made the earth shake and caused the weakened wall above us to rock. Yellow earth and grey smoke rose up from four points along the enemy trench. Then, finally, it got too much for the British. They took to their heels and ran backwards as fast as their legs could carry them.

Nobody gave an order on our side, but almost everyone rushed out of our houses, shouting Hurra! It would in fact have been better had we stayed where we were and simply fired from there, because our shells were still landing in the enemy trench. But who could show such control at a time like that? Then, suddenly, I received an awful blow to the left shoulder, causing me to cry out as I was thrown forwards. I was gasping for breath, my heart was beating fit to burst, my fingers clawed at the grass, my teeth ground together and my right foot came up against a metal object, which I saw later was my bayonet which was lying behind me. I realised that I had been shot in the back by a bullet which had exited through my chest and I thought that my last hour had come. Soon things improved a little. I could breathe once more and my heart rate steadied. I shouted to the man next to me to take my knapsack off. The rear of it was already soaked in blood. Extraordinary to relate, my next thought was, 'Well, you will be spending Christmas at home'.

Meanwhile, further south, German pressure against 1st (Cavalry) Division on **30 October**, mainly through heavy shelling, had its reward in the sense that the British withdrew to a new line, from north of Messines to in front of Wytschaete, now more or less on the crest of the ridge, and then across to the Comines Canal forward of St Eloi. In general this move was done with few casualties, though the 57th lost the majority of a company at Oostaverne as did the 129th, which had been sent forward to cover the withdrawal. 4th Division to the south, before Ploegsteert Wood, retained all its positions.

The seriousness of the situation had led to Haig calling upon the French for assistance before midday and again, rather more urgently, at 3 pm. General Dubois, commanding the French IX Corps, sent up two cavalry brigades (one of these to Hooge) as well as three infantry battalions, concentrated near Zillebeke. A further battalion was sent up shortly before midnight. In fact none of these troops were called upon to hold the line on the 30th; but their presence must have brought considerable reassurance both to commanders and their men. French managed to find some men to send as well, a territorial unit, the London Scottish. The intention was for a counter attack early next morning, both north and south of the canal. However, with a night attack against Messines launched at about 10 pm, Allenby instructed his 1st Division to remain on the defensive.

As night fell on the first day of operations by Army Group Fabeck, it appeared that the fears expressed by Oberstleutnant Fritz von Loßberg had been well founded. Here and there were signs of success, but the outcome largely fell short of expectations. As has been described, formations of XV Corps captured Zandvoorde and its chateau; but on the right flank, the failure of XXVII Reserve Corps to take Gheluvelt had a knock on effect and there was very little progress. Conscious of

French troops moving up to the line.

Zandvoorde after the battle.

the need to get forward, Commander XV Corps (General der Infanterie von Deimling) tried to persuade Fabeck to allocate to him the heavy howitzers of 2nd Battalion Mörser Regiment 3, which were being held in reserve near Comines, but Fabeck decided to give three of the four available batteries to II Bavarian Corps in the *Schwerpunkt*, so XV Corps had to manage with the services of only one battery. Deimling then attempted to intervene in the Gheluvelt area, but even the deployment of several battalions attacking in that direction failed to alter the situation; the village continuing for the time being to hold out. 26th Infantry Division from Württemberg, commanded by Duke Wilhelm of Urach, operating in the extreme south of the Army Group sector, spent the day locked into tough fighting in an area which lent itself far more to defensive operations than attack.

The Battle for Messines (1st Cavalry Division): 30th October
The defence of Messines was principally the task of de Lisle's 1st (Cavalry) Division; to the south, beyond the Douve, that of 4th Division (although it gradually extended its front northwards as the day progressed). As can be seen from the map, the line around Messines was a pronounced salient to the east in the general direction of the British line, a consequence of falling back from positions further north the previous day. **(See map p. 64)**

The history of 11/Hussars describes Messines and its importance:

> *It was a small village with about fourteen hundred inhabitants and there was nothing very notable about its buildings except that the church was a fine old Norman building dating from the eleventh century* [the abbey, of which the church formed part, was founded in 1057]. *The main street ran almost due north south and carried the main road from Ypres to Armentières. In the middle of the village, opening out of the main street to the east, was a small square. In the south east corner of the village stood the church and next to it was a convent which was surrounded by a high wall. A few dozen yards outside the village on the east was a brick works with a number of brick stacks. ... The important feature about Messines was its position ... it rises about one hundred and fifty feet above the level of the surrounding countryside and is a formidable barrier to any army that wishes to pass south of Ypres either from the east or the west. ... In a word, the village of Messines stands in a commanding position and affords splendid observation, facts which explain the importance with which it was regarded by both sides throughout nearly four years of war.*

Messines Church and the Institution Royale before the battle.

On the evening of 30 October, I (Cavalry) Brigade covered the area. The defenders of this large village (in fact the smallest town in Belgium) comprised the 9/Lancers under Lieutenant Colonel David Campbell [who in due course went on to command 21st Division], actually part of 2 Brigade. His 150 men were supported on his right by Indian troops, two companies of the 57th, and on his left by the Queen's Bays; 11/Hussars manned the support line in the village itself, having been withdrawn from the front line after the fighting of the 30th, whilst the remaining regiment in the brigade, the 5th Dragoon Guards (5/DG) were split between the support and front lines.

Situation at Messines on the evening of 30 October.

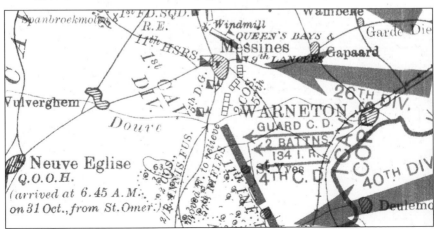

The 57th were to be withdrawn in the early hours and replaced by 2/Inniskilling Fusiliers of 12 Brigade. All through the evening and night there had been sporadic shelling by German howitzers and sniping from cover as close as a hundred yards from the British lines. Whilst the relief of the 57th was in progress, sometime around 4.30 am, the Germans attacked Messines and the areas immediately north and south of it.

The biggest problems for the British defences came to the south of the village. A demonstration was made against the sections of trench - there was no complete trench system – between the Douve and the village. A company of 2/Inniskilling had only just occupied these. This was almost immediately followed by an assault – 'cheering and with horns blowing' – on the south eastern defences of the village, at that stage still manned by the 57th. Some Germans crossed the trenches and attacked the support trench, manned by 5/DG. The enemy was despatched or driven back, though others managed to bypass these defences by going around on the left of them. These were pushed back by the men of the 57th, recently relieved by 2/Inniskilling, though at the expense of the loss of their commander, Captain RS Gordon. (Strange to say, the CWGC shows his date of death as 29 October.) Other Germans who had managed to get over the support line were halted by a barricade further in the village manned by C Squadron 5/DG.

The German Field Artillery Regiments 29 and 65, firing in support of this preliminary assault, had great problems; difficulties that were magnified for the batteries in direct support of the forward battalions. The regimental historian of Field Artillery Regiment 29 later quoted from the words of an anonymous diarist who was present on 30 October.

One section [of guns] *had to be advanced even further so as to provide intimate support to the infantry. If the reconnaissance itself was very problematic, the move of the guns into position demanded an even more amazing performance by the gunners. They had to wade knee deep in the mud, whilst the guns themselves sank in up to their axles - and all this was achieved under constant artillery and small arms fire. The daring troop was hindered especially by the fire of some machine guns but, finally, Reserve Vizewachtmeister Engländer succeeded in locating these troublemakers and a few well directed shells silenced them. However, in order to be able to engage the main enemy trenches, it was necessary to change positions again.*

Everyone set to work with a will. Making use of long tow ropes, the guns were hauled through deep boggy ground, over churned up tracks and deep, sharp sided, trenches. The section was now a mere three hundred metres from the enemy. Right and left the infantry were poised to launch the assault. Two men worked the guns. Everyone else slithered backwards and forwards under heavy rifle and machine gun fire fetching ammunition and the guns were fired at the fastest rate possible. The enemy did not hold out for long. To shouts of Hurra! the infantry advanced and captured the enemy position.

This description concerns the attack on the British advanced defensive positions and not on Messines itself, which was not finally cleared until 1 November. One of the main problems was the fact that the regiments of 26th Infantry Division, having had to march previously to Menin and Geluwe (not to be confused with Gheluvelt) immediately after a seventy two hour battle for Fromelles, then had to move all the way forward via Quesnoy and Warneton to positions about two kilometres east of Messines. It does not require much imagination to see that by the time they relieved elements of the German 6th Cavalry Division, late on 29 October, they were nearing exhaustion and required above all a period of rest; certainly not an assault against a target as difficult to take as Messines. Much as a break might have been needed, the pressure of events and the need to conform to the remainder of Army Group Fabeck, meant that every sinew had to be stretched even to be on the start line on time; there was no time available for systematic preparation or even the most rudimentary reconnaissance.

The auguries were not good. However, it was at least discovered that the main British defensive line was established about one kilometre to the east of Messines along a ridge running away towards Wambeke. It was obvious that the defenders enjoyed excellent fields of fire, whereas the attackers would be able to find little in the way of covered approaches or cover from view or fire. There were a few ditches and hedges and a scattering of buildings but all in all it was dispiriting prospect for the tired men from Württemberg. Dominating the entire battlefield was the brooding presence of Messines perched atop the ridge to which it gave its name.

The bombardment of the British positions and of Messines itself had begun early on 30 October. This drew immediate counter fire from British batteries located near Messines and Wambeke. However, the See map p. 69 weight of fire was insufficient to prevent the formations of 26th Infantry Division from setting out for their objectives but the attack soon encountered major problems. Fusilier Regiment 122 headed directly towards Wambeke and Infantry Regiment 125 for Messines and they ran into trouble only a short time later. 1st Battalion Infantry Regiment 125, commanded by Hauptmann Müller, aiming for Blauwepoorthoek, came under a torrent of fire from directly ahead and off on the right flank. This not only caused the attack to stall, the company out on the right flank had to withdraw into cover. 2nd Battalion Infantry Regiment 125 ran into similar problems as it pressed forward to Messines. This time the small arms fire came from the north, somewhere near Wytschaete. The direct support batteries switched all their fire onto Messines, but the strength of the buildings was proof against the fire of field guns and it was no easy task to redirect the fire of the heavy howitzers onto the target. For the time being the attack was completely stalled.

Shortly before 2.00 pm the commanding officer 2nd Battalion Infantry Regiment 125, Major Sproesser, reported, 'My impression is that the attack is still not sufficiently prepared. Enemy rifle and machine gun fire from the area northwest of Les Quatre Rois is still coming down with undiminished force.' In actual fact, it was more or less at that moment that Fusilier Regiment 122 succeeded in making some ground and, for a time, it appeared as though it might be possible to reinvigorate the attack. Unfortunately the friction of war and typically problematic 1914 command and control combined to mean that the opportunity was lost. The commander, Infantry Regiment 125, took the decision to renew the attack against Messines at about 2.00 pm, the same time that 51 Infantry Brigade ordered precisely the same thing. By the time the brigade order had reached Infantry Regiment 125, it was already 4.55 pm, by which time the renewed attack, lacking sufficient artillery support, had already failed. Major Sproesser's report, timed at 4.00 pm, stated, 'Under fire from infantry and artillery to the front and machine guns in the right flank, 2nd Battalion Infantry Regiment 125 cannot get forward'. The fundamental problem was that (just as the chief of staff Army Group Fabeck, Oberstleutnant Loßberg, had predicted), a spirited defence conducted in terrain that was very much in its favour caused endless delays and confusion, so momentum was lost.

As described above, British reinforcements were brought up, four squadrons worth, from 5/DG, 11th Hussars and 4/DG of 2 Brigade; whilst 2/Inniskilling launched a counter attack from their positions south of Messines. As it became lighter, the Germans fell back, now also subject to enfilade fire from 4th Division's artillery on Hill 63. All that had been achieved by the attack was the abandonment of the firing line to the south east of the village, originally held by the 57th. Elsewhere, to the centre and north of the village, this initial attack made no progress. But there was far more to come.

The small number of British prisoners of war, approximately three hundred from the British 4th and 7th Divisions, together with a few cavalrymen, was an indicator of how slow progress had been on 30 October; though the fact that the main clashes had tended to be against outpost lines was a further significant factor. It was also apparent that Messines, Wytschaete and Gheluvelt seemed to be held in significant strength. To add to concern on the German side, there were air reconnaissance reports that day, showing that strong reinforcements were assembled between Ypres and Poperinghe and that there was a great deal of rail traffic forward from Dunkirk in the direction of Hazebrouck. Bearing in mind that the advance on 30 October had not met expectations, this news was far from welcome for senior German commanders. It was evident that every effort had to be made to put the defence under pressure and speed up the capture of Messines Ridge.

31st October

This date is famous in British military history for the battle around Gheluvelt. However, the German attack to capture Messines Ridge and the high ground beyond remained a crucial part of the overall plan to overwhelm the allied troops in the Ypres area. Even the Kaiser had arrived in the neighbourhood to provide his moral support for what was hoped would be a vital – if not decisive – blow to bring the war on the western front to a speedy conclusion.

One problem that the Germans faced was that of poor intelligence. There was a fear that a number of Britain's fourteen territorial divisions (which existed at least on paper) were lurking undetected and this may go some way to explain the relative cautious approach made, for example, of the successes of the previous day. The *OH* becomes almost lyrical in its review of the day's fighting, commenting on the perceived view that the Germans now had of facing an exhausted enemy:

> *A decisive victory seemed assured: for everything pointed to the British being completely exhausted. And they may well have appeared so to the enemy. The line that stood between the British Empire and ruin was composed of tired, haggard and unshaven men, unwashed, plastered with mud, many in little more than rags. But they had their guns, rifles and bayonets, and, at any rate, plenty of rifle ammunition, whilst the artillerymen always managed to have rounds available at the right place at critical moments.*

Despite general exhaustion amongst the German infantry, 26th Infantry Division set about exploiting the hours of darkness to resupply, reorganise tangled units and prepare the way for a resumption of the advance the following day. This plan, which also allowed a certain amount of rest for the weary troops, was thrown into disarray at midnight when orders arrived from 51 Infantry Brigade directing a night attack against Messines, with an H Hour of 1.45 am. Every single reserve that could be found was sent forward to reinforce it and to allow an exhausted Bavarian Reserve Jäger Battalion to withdraw to Gapaard. It was greatly to the credit of the formations of the division that the attack could actually be launched as planned. Good training and a concerted effort saw the Brigade attacking as directed; this time with the benefit of fire support from the heavy howitzers, which had been redeployed earlier. The small British garrison, comprising elements of 1st Cavalry Brigade, reinforced by the 9th Lancers of 2nd Cavalry Brigade and two companies of the Indian 57th Rifles fought hard, but they faced tall odds. Ground was gained slowly. There were checks and minor reverses but by mid morning 1st and 3rd Battalions Infantry Regiment 125 had forced their way into the outskirts of Messines and were starting to consolidate their positions.

The assault on Messines 30/31 October.

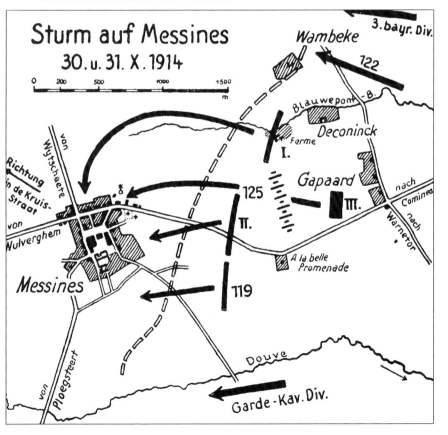

At 9.20 am two companies of 3rd Battalion Infantry Regiment 121 under Major Menzel arrived and were thrown into the battle. With the arrival of these extra forces, Infantry Regiment 125 continued to press forward. One particularly stubborn barricade on the road to Gapaard was stormed by a party from 10th Company under Feldwebel Marx. Having breached this, the remainder of the company charged forward and managed to fight its way into houses right on the edge of the village. Despite this, there were still pockets of resistance and further barricades in the village. A concerted effort was being made during the early afternoon to clear all of these, when the commander Infantry Regiment 125, Generalmajor von Martin, arrived to oversee the battle. The combination of determined resistance and the friction inherent in costly street fighting led to a long drawn out struggle as one barricade or strongpoint after another had to be attacked and captured, with fire support at very close range from single manhandled guns of Field Artillery Regiment 29. Hauptmann Heinrich of the gunner regiment, supported by a team from 5th Company Infantry Regiment 125 led by Leutnant Wanner, distinguished themselves in this close quarter battle; an attack which was further supported by the Machine Gun Company, which leapfrogged its guns forward from one captured building to another, there to bring down overhead fire from the upstairs windows. A letter from a German infantryman, quoted in 11/Hussars' history, found its way into a Stuttgart newspaper in early November:

We relieved them (the dismounted cavalry) during the night of 29/30 in pouring rain. At first we remained lying quietly in our trenches – the right wing was still too far back – but afterwards, towards evening [30 October]*, we proceeded to attack, the task set to our regiment being to take Messines. The night fell while we were still advancing slowly. The English were firing as hard as they could, with the result that we had to fall back some distance. Further advance in the night was impossible against the hellish fire; we dug ourselves in, but had to be keenly on the alert, so as not to be surprised by a counter thrust of the English.*

At daybreak we continued our attack and, with the aid of the artillery, we succeeded after a hard fight, in driving the English out of their trenches into the village. Of course, we pressed after them, and occupied the eastern outskirts of Messines. Here a terrible struggle ensued, in which the English fought in a way to compel our highest respect, at least as regards their soldierly qualities. In the village itself they had occupied every house, the streets were barred by barricades – metres in thickness, the windows of the houses stuffed up with sandbags, the doors barricaded with furniture and stones; through the walls they drilled loopholes scarcely visible; each house was a small fortress, scattering death and destruction. In the midst of the firing we made a breach in the first barricade and penetrated with fixed bayonets into the empty village street. Right and left of us a thousand bullets were whistling ominously; here and there one of our men fell. With our hatchet-picks we knocked holes into the walls of the houses, through which we entered to clear the next. Thus we succeeded in penetrating to about a depth of fifty metres into the village, until we were brought to a stop by the next barricade. All at once machine gun fire was opened upon us from immediately behind on the left. There is no help for it – all take refuge in the houses, in the road ditches and behind the barricade. What was to be done? We indeed took some more houses by again breaking through the walls, but afterwards even this was no longer feasible; anyone showing himself in the road was shot down.

The British garrison, though not especially strong had, nevertheless, inflicted a considerable number of casualties on 26th Infantry Division. By the middle of the afternoon Grenadier Regiment 119 and Infantry

A pre war photograph of the officers of Grenadier Regiment 119, the senior regiment of the army of Württemberg.

Regiment 125, which had spearheaded the assault and by then had been in action for almost ten hours, were in urgent need of relief or at least reinforcement. However, one of the reasons that Infantry Regiment 121 had been kept back in reserve was its cumulative previous losses around Fromelles. Its 11th Company, for example, was down to only three junior NCOs and thirty men and was in no fit state for a further period of intensive fighting. Nevertheless, it soon sent 9th Company to Grenadier Regiment 119, followed shortly by 5th and 8th Companies, then amalgamated 10th and 11th Companies and despatched them to Infantry Regiment 125.

The British account of the day tells of desperate fighting against the odds. With daylight, and after the early morning mist had lifted somewhat on 31 October, German heavy howitzers and other artillery were concentrated on the village followed, an hour later, at 9.00 am, with a renewed assault by the 26th Division. Once more the main thrust of the attack was on the two flanks, north and south, of Messines. The

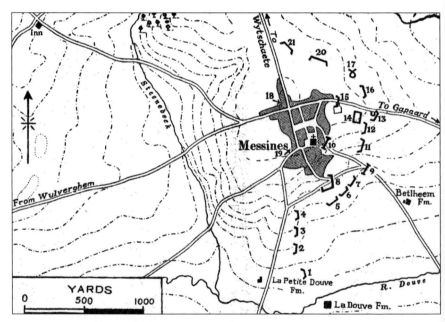

The Defence of Messines 31 October.

bombardment had already caused significant damage to the houses, whilst sniping and machine gun fire had taken its toll of the defenders. 9/Lancers, defending the eastern face, were withdrawn through the support line, held by 11/Hussars; this line was now connected with that of the Queen's Bays to the north and 2/Inniskilling to the south and thus removed the pronounced salient in the line. Once more the attack was fended off.

A further attack followed about an hour later, with at least one gun brought right forward to assist in clearing the houses of defenders. By midday the British line had fallen back to the line of the main Ypres road, in the western half of the village. At this stage reinforcements arrived from II Corps. II Corps had been engaged in the fighting south of Armentières but was being relieved on 30 October. French ordered a composite brigade, consisting of 1/Northumberland Fusiliers (1/NF), 1/Lincolns, 2/KOSB and 2/KOYLI, to be sent to Neuve Eglise, under the command of Brigadier General Shaw, and to come under Allenby's control. This brigade had already moved up behind Kemmel and Allenby asked for 2/KOSB – with a total of only some 300 men (but see below) - and 2/KOYLI – with some 350 - to be sent to Messines.

They now became part of a general counter attack, begun at about 1 pm, by infantry around Messines. To the north, the London Scottish, about whom more later, pushed forward over the Wytschaete road; 2/KOYLI advanced north of and 2/KOSB south of the Wulverghem road (both battalions, according to the *OH*, only in the region of 300 men strong), whilst 2/Inniskilling came across from south of the village. The latter regained the lost trenches of the 57th, but little progress was made in the village, though 2/KSOB did manage to retake the convent (Institute Royale), south of the church.

2/KOSB on the morning of 31 October had actually been recovering in Merville from its efforts in the fighting around La Bassée and absorbing a draft of eighty three men, which still left its strength at only just over 600 – note the divergence with the figure from the Official History; it is possible that a significant number were left behind. Up and about shortly after 3 am, by 6.30 am they were in buses up to Wulverghem via Wytschaete, where the battalion was instructed to advance (which commenced at 1 pm) up the Wulverghem road, with 2/KOYLI to the north – a combined reinforcement of some 800 men.

It was desperate close fighting. Sometimes only fifty yards or less separated the foes. House to house fighting is as difficult to describe as it is to conduct. ... In that most nerve-stretching, surprising type of warfare, when death may threaten from above, below, at the side and even from behind, the KOSB took the convent and cleaned out the houses near the church. But though the enemy was seen hurrying back to his prepared positions by the brickfields, east of Messines, once he got there, by covering fire from his reserves, he was able to hold the KOSB within the eastern edge.

2/KOYLI had had less time to recover from the fighting around Richebourg l'Avoué, only coming out of the line in the early hours of the 30th after a nine day stint in which the battalion had over 300 casualties, including one of the two officers and a significant number of a draft of 149 men which had arrived on the 25th. The battalion was also transported by bus and joined in the move to reinforce the troops in Messines.

However, it was found that the western [eastern?] portion of the village was still in the enemy's hands, and that he had collected machine guns there; the reception that the attacking companies met with rendered a further advance impractical until our artillery should have time in which to destroy the houses in which these machine guns were mounted. The trenches were therefore not retaken, but the battalion dug itself in under a devastating fire. By 2 pm the supporting companies and the remnants of B and C Companies had entrenched themselves and were prepared to hold the line of the road running north south through Messines. Casualties were very heavy ...

By 6 pm, Captain Carter was left in command [he was the surviving officer from the draft of 25 October]. *He requested the CO of the London Scottish to fill a gap between his men* [who were to the northern end of Messines] *and the Carabiniers; when this was done the line, though much attenuated, was made continuous, if scarcely to be called solid.*

The troops were too few and already fatigued from their experiences of the last days on top of the tiring approach, which had been under German shell fire from an early stage. However, the intervention by this injection of infantry was sufficient for 1st Division to hold its new line. The Germans had superiority in numbers and artillery, but street fighting is difficult at the best of times and, as evening approached, it is more than likely that Germans ended up shooting at each other. To the south they made little progress, exposed as that flank was to fire from British positions west of Ploegsteert Wood and the higher ground to the north of it; north of the village they failed to secure the top of the ridge.

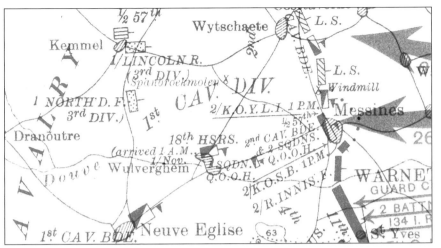

Situation at Messines on the evening of 31 October.

The London Scottish – or 14th London Regiment – were the first infantry territorial unit to go into action; unlike most of the army, they were still organised in eight companies instead of the usual four. Since September, on arrival in France, they had come under GHQ control and were employed as lines of communication troops. They had had a very busy twenty four hours; despatched to Haig by French, to assist with his 'puttying up' of the line, i.e. securing gaps in it, they had arrived in Hooge and formed part of I Corps reserve, but not for long. Almost immediately, during the night of the 30th, they were ordered back to Ypres and from there were to be transported, famously, in buses to the Cavalry Corps area. Allenby attached the battalion to the 2nd Division and they were sent to St Eloi. However, with developments at Messines, they were given to the 1st Division.

De Lisle did not direct the battalion to the direct defence of Messines but determined to have it available for a counter attack – unscathed by

A soldier of the London Scottish in the uniform worn at Messines in 1914.

fighting, it had 750 men in its ranks. He ordered it to move to the front of 4 Brigade and to move via Wytschaete and the windmill on the Messines-Wytschaete road. It was then to attack the Germans, moving south eastwards, in conjunction with 4 Brigade, at about noon. Because Wytschaete was under such heavy fire, the battalion used the cover of the western side of the ridge and moved to L'Enfer Wood, north west of the windmill. From here it was ordered by 4 Brigade commander to reinforce the cavalry line (mainly 6/DG) on the far side of the road. Assuming that they were being deployed to stem an attack, the battalion advanced as though to launch a counter attack. If they had acted as though reinforcing the line, they would have 'dribbled' (as the *OH* puts it) forward,

GA Malcolm, CO of the London Scottish at Messines, here pictured as a colonel.

thereby saving numerous casualties that their chosen formation produced, for they were observed by the Germans and were shelled heavily. They came up on the Brigade's right and some men engaged in fighting with Germans on the left. They also had to endure a particular problem with their newly issued rifles, as the regimental history relates:

About 9 pm [31 October] *the Germans attempted their first attack on the ridge. They came on all along the front, cheering loudly and with their bands playing. But they were driven back by the rifle fire and were nowhere able to close on the position. The dense mass in which the enemy advanced gave splendid targets at short range in the moonlight and there were many expert shots in the London Scottish firing line, so the loss of the Bavarians who were up against them must have been serious. It would have been heavier still if the battalion had been better armed. The new rifles, served out the day before leaving Abbots Langley, proved to be defective. There had been no opportunity for rifle practice after landing in France and not a man in the battalion had ever fired a shot from his new rifle until he used it in battle. The rifles were the Mark I converted to take Mark VII ammunition. Not till the battalion was in action was it discovered that the magazine had too weak a spring, and its front clips were of the wrong shape for the Mark VII bullet. This caused refusal of the cartridge to enter the chamber of the barrel, for either the point of the bullet came too low and hit the lower part of the breech entrance and jammed there, or it jumped and hit the top of the breech entrance,*

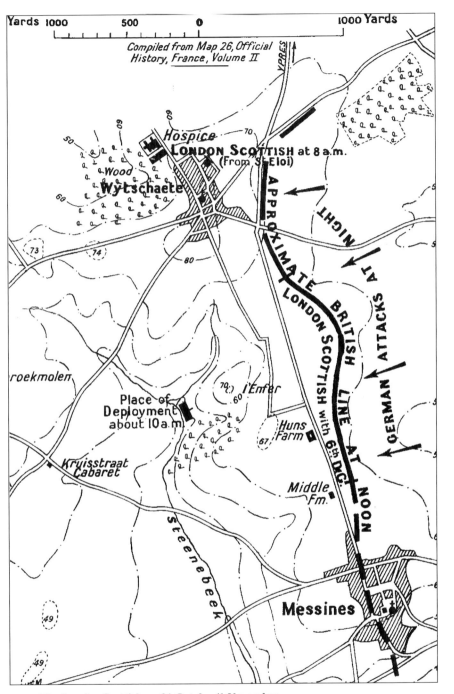

The London Scottish on 31 October/1 November.

77

sometimes breaking off the point of the bullet. It was certainly a serious matter for men opening fire in their first battle to find their rifles jamming and the magazine failing to act. The magazines were useless and the rifles had to be used as single loaders. All the same, steady shooting beat off the attack.

The bombardment of the ridge began again and continued till after midnight. By this time the full moon had risen high and the windmill [the location of the regimental memorial today] *in the Scottish centre and Huns Farm towards their left were on fire. In the glare of this light the Germans attacked again. There was a great burst of cheering, their band struck up 'Deutschland, Deutschland über Alles', and they came on in dense waves. For more than an hour they were held at bay; rush after rush was stopped by the fire from the Scottish front, but the enemy came on again and again. At last the attack seemed to exhaust itself, and there was a lull, but towards 2 am* [1 November] *the enemy came on again, and this time drove their attack home.*

Lieutenant Colonel Arthur Dugdale, Oxfordshire Hussars, who was unusual in commanding his regiment throughout the war.

That night 1 (Cavalry) Brigade, which suffered twenty five officer – a very high proportion – and 169 other rank casualties during 31 October, was relieved by 2 Brigade. It was not a very convincing defensive line; for example, 2/KOSB only had one officer remaining,

Val Fleming DSO MP.

Captain Guy Bonham-Carter, killed in action in May 1915.

but the situation did not differ from much of the severely stressed line before Ypres. **(See map p. 83)**

Amongst the units that took part in the relief were the Oxfordshire Hussars, which had just arrived at the front after several weeks of duties behind the lines. Being a territorial unit, it had some personalities who had an impact in civilian life. For example, Val Fleming DSO was the MP for South Oxfordshire; he was killed in a German attack on Gillemont Farm in May 1917 and is buried in Templeux le Guerard British Cemetery, E 40. His main claim to fame is that he was father of the creator of James Bond, Ian Fleming. Guy Bonham-Carter was a scion of that famous family; he was killed in May 1915 and is buried at Vlamertinghe Cemetery, I G 3. The regiment fought at Messines, mainly acting as a reserve to the west of the ridge.

31 October/1 November

Elements of 26th Infantry Division spent the night 31 October/1 November under cover in well-constructed buildings on the edge of Messines, though Reserve Leutnant Mößner and his platoon managed, despite the streets being swept by British fire, to infiltrate as far as the main square and to occupy a dominating building there. Generalmajor von Martin, who it will be recalled arrived the previous afternoon to take personal command of the operation, decided that a final effort to secure Messines was to be made as soon as possible. At 5.50 am, he issued this order:

> *1st Battalion is to bypass the northern edge of Messines, then advance astride the Wytschaete - Messines road, occupying the northern edge, front facing west and go into defence.*
>
> *3rd Battalion, with two platoons of machine guns* [four guns], *one howitzer and half a platoon of engineers, is to advance astride the Gapaard – Wulverghem road, straight through Messines so as to occupy its western edge and go into defence there.*
>
> *2nd Battalion, with one platoon of machine guns, one howitzer and half a platoon of engineers, is to advance on the market square, cross it and advance along the road to Ploegsteert, until the western edge is reached, where it is to go into defence.*
>
> *Battalion Menzel remains at my disposal.*

At 6.00 am, the first of the howitzers of Field Artillery Regiment 65 opened fire on the thick walls. It was virtually a suicide mission for the howitzer crews, because they immediately attracted heavy small arms and artillery fire from the defence, but they continued to fire, even when casualties began to amount alarmingly. Gradually the defenders began to pull back and the German infantry fought their way forward, helped considerably by the howitzers firing at point blank range and the fire of Mößner's men, which raked the market square continuously.

A report in a subsequent Württemberg edition of the *Liller Zeitung* carried an eyewitness account of the battle.

> *The thunderous roar of the guns in the village streets made an appalling noise. The houses hit by them were blown apart, crashing down as smoke and dust pillared upwards. The musketiers followed closely in the wake of the guns, which fired shell after shell, pushing forward over debris and corpses until the last gunner, its courageous commander, fell seriously wounded.*

Casualties were generally heavy throughout the action due to the close quarter house to house fighting but, by the end of the morning, thanks in part to decisive work by Leutnant Schröder, commanding 10th Company Infantry Regiment 121, who led an assault on the northern edge of the village, reports reached Generalmajor von Martin that his orders had been carried out in full.

Infantry Regiment 125 dug in west of the village, Menzel's companies to the south and the very next day Martin, heading a long list of regimental medal winners, was awarded an immediate Iron Cross First Class. Messines itself was a scene of virtually total destruction. Its religious buildings were in ruins as was the *Institution Royale* (identified by the Germans as being, 'for the daughters of officers'). Leutnant

General der Infanterie Karl Ritter von Martin, Commander II Bavarian Army Corps.

Schröder, who was in charge of the *ad hoc* amalgamated company which played a key part in the battle, later described how events unfurled in Messines that day. The main threads of his story dovetail well with what is known from the British perspective.

> *The little village of Messines stood out on the hill to our front like an old fortress on a mountain top. Of course it had no battlements or towers set into its walls but, nevertheless, torrents of fire from concealed trenches and loopholes poured down on the daring attackers who were attempting to storm the heights.*

Despite this, our neighbouring regiment had succeeded in closing right up to the edge of village from where, out of hastily dug holes, they were conducting a costly fire fight. It was essential to capture the broad sweep of terrain in front of the dominant village, but a frontal attack would have been difficult to carry out and a flanking attack [against the northern end of the village] promised greater success.

10th Company, which was dug in on the flank in the second line, was ordered by 51 Infantry Brigade at about midday on 31 October to move over to the right and to take the village in the flank by means of a swift charge. This was a serious mission, because the British had prepared every house for defence. Moving individually or in small groups, the riflemen sprang up out of their trenches and made their way in bounds forward and to the right. This was carried out amidst rapid rifle and machine gun fire and the whole area was also under shrapnel fire. Rushing forward, creeping and crawling in cover behind hedges and garden fences, the riflemen reached the cover of a small hollow.

Many, including the company commander (who was wounded), had already been hit, but it was essential to press on. To the front of the left flank platoon a small ditch ran directly towards a tile works [The Brickstacks], which was strongly defended. Everybody piled into the ditch, the platoon commander leading and soon they were about sixty metres from the tile works. A quick order was given and the platoon dashed forward as one at the double, shouting Hurra! and entered the yard. The British left in great haste and the building was swiftly prepared for defence.

The other platoons, advancing in a similar manner, had pushed up against the northern exit to the village and stormed the first of the houses in the face of lacerating fire, which tore holes in their ranks. Messages were sent back requesting reinforcements and ammunition but, instead, the British counter attacked. The aim was to drive out these people who had forced their way in, threatening their flank and rear, but they did not make much progress and they were sent back home with bloody heads. Darkness fell, supports came up and, with them, two guns. Assisted by some of our men these were quickly brought into action out on the street. They fired at occupied houses and street barricades with great effect, but the British artillery, unconcerned about their men in the village, brought down heavy fire. This cost

Messines after the battle.

us casualties during the night, including the battery commander [Hauptmann Heuß, 6th Battery Field Artillery Regiment 65], *who was killed. However, the British dared not attack. Messines had been taken, admittedly with heavy losses, thanks to the energetic flanking attack of the 10th Company.*

The Capture of Hollebeke Chateau and The Defence of Wytschaete, 2nd (Cavalry) Division 31 October.

Elsewhere II Bavarian Corps, operating in the *Schwerpunkt* of the German offensive, had been enjoying more success on 30 October, though overall progress was still somewhat disappointing. 4th Bavarian Division (Generalleutnant Graf von Montgelas), finally overran Hollebeke at about 3.30 pm after heavy fighting over a period of hours, but the area around the chateau itself held out until late evening. Further south, 3rd Bavarian Division (Generalleutnant Ritter von Breitkopf), manoeuvring in tandem with 26th Infantry Division from Württemberg (Generalleutnant Wilhelm Duke of Urach), advanced west of Wambeke to a line approximately two kilometres short of the crest of the Messines

Generalleutnant Ritter von Breitkopf, Commander 3rd Bavarian Infantry Division.

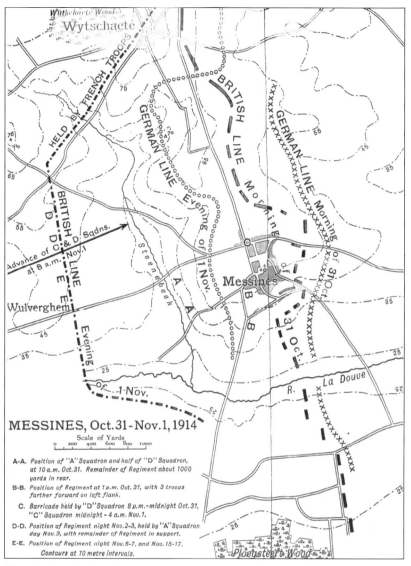

Situation at Messines 31 October - 1 November (Oxfordshire Hussars).

Ridge, whilst 26th Infantry Division was able to get to within 1,200 metres of Wytschaete.

Meanwhile elements of both 3rd and 4th Bavarian Infantry Divisions were involved in intense fighting for the Hollebeke area. Hollebeke Chateau to the east of the village and the Ypres - Comines railway was an important objective, as was a second chateau, known as the White Chateau, which was located just south of the Ypres - Comines canal about 1,500 metres northwest of Hollebeke itself. Bavarian Infantry Regiment 9, with 1st Bavarian Jäger Battalion and Infantry Regiment 172 of 39th Infantry Division to its right, continued to press on towards the high ground west of Zandvoorde, but Bavarian Infantry Regiment 5 was completely entangled in the battle for Hollebeke Chateau. Artillery direct support was provided by two batteries of field guns and Bavarian Infantry Regiment 5 initially launched an attack on a two battalion frontage. This soon began to stall and by the middle of the day the commander had to deploy his own third battalion and one company from Bavarian Jäger Battalion 2 forward. This

Generalleutnant Graf von Montgelas, Commander Bavarian 4th Infantry Division.

additional support enabled it to close in on the chateau and to take a number of prisoners, including a captain and two troopers from the King's Dragoon Guards.

Bavarian Infantry Regiment 17 of 3rd Bavarian Infantry Division, which was directly involved in the battle for the White Chateau – not to

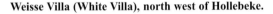

Weisse Villa (White Villa), north west of Hollebeke.

be confused with Hollebeke Chateau, used different tactics, advancing on a narrow front and overran a series of machine gun and section positions by means of minor platoon and company tactics. This was inevitably a slow process, so it was well after 9.00 pm and pitch black by the time formations of 6 Bavarian Infantry Brigade seized and controlled the area around the White Chateau. A vivid but, at times, tiresomely overblown, account of his service with Bavarian Infantry Regiment 17 entitled *Mit Hurra in den Tod!* was written after the war by Reserve Leutnant Hermann Kohl. In his account of events that day, he refers to 'Hollebeke Chateau', but he was mistaken. He was involved in the fight for the imposing White Chateau.

Oberst Georg Meyer, Commander Bavarian Infantry Regiment 17, pictured later as a generalmajor.

The German assault flooded northwest towards Hollebeke. Blow after blow was struck, but enemy machine guns fired mercilessly and tore holes in the ranks. We were up against the same sort of fanatical opponents we had met at Maricourt. Here they clung on like glue to their ground and refused to yield one single square metre voluntarily. Charge followed charge as the companies crashed in. Bronzed Indian troops lay there, cut down in rows. They were Herculean men, with complete contempt for death, who took not a single step backwards! They preferred to die where they were! Only over their shattered skulls could the sacred charger of Mars advance to victory! Their fearful wrath as they faced death was matched only by the anger burning in the hearts of the German ranks.

Towards 4.00 pm Wibel's Battalion [Major Moritz Wibel, commanding officer 2nd Battalion] *had pushed the attack to within three hundred metres of Hollebeke, Haasy's Battalion* [Major Wilhelm von Haasy, commanding officer 3rd Battalion] *had crossed the canal and was advancing on the final objective of the day. It was tough, bitter, fighting. The potential of every building, right up to its rafters, was cunningly exploited for its defensive possibilities, the dense woods served as one long endless barrier to progress. Fire blazed down from the treetops, serving its deadly veto on the Bavarians storming forward … It was fighting at its hardest and only the good Lord knew to whom the evening would belong.*

The German guns roared, hurling their smashing steel with

85

White Chateau, Hollebeke.

religious fervour, like a raging storm ... but one battery fired using incorrect sight settings and hit the rear of Haasy's Battalion badly. With dull thuds German shells came down amongst our own ranks. The commander gave the sign and the trumpeters blew 'Halt!' The battle was paused as runners raced back to the battery position but then, fifteen minutes later, a new performance took centre stage. There was an overture of the loudest fortissimo and the battle entered its final phase. The enemy line crumbled and, at 3.30 pm Hollebeke, that blood-soaked bulwark, was in German hands.

This success was a spur to further action. That evening, despite being worn out by the battles of the day, the Bavarian 17th, in conjunction with the neighbouring troops, stormed the grounds of Hollebeke Chateau [ie White Chateau]. *The German Hurra! came like a shot out of the distance, echoed off the walls of the chateau and shook the occupants out of their carefree existence. In a tearing hurry, the enemy staff vacated the chateau, abandoning a freshly laid table, complete with silver cutlery and every delicacy. It must have been painful for that Great Nation to leave such sumptuous food to the barbarians, but the Germans were to have no problem dealing with it.*

From the German perspective, the capture of the two chateaux near Hollebeke was a key development. General Ritter von Martini was thereafter able to direct II Bavarian Corps to continue to press on in a northwesterly direction, but to switch its main effort to the Messines –

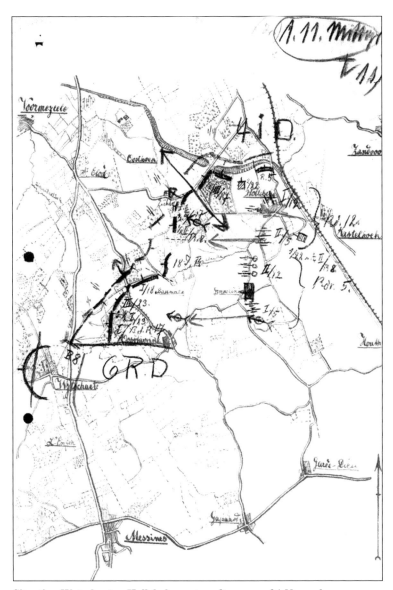

Situation Wytschaete - Hollebeke sector afternoon of 1 November.

Wytschaete ridge and to manoeuvre so as to the deploy the previously uncommitted regiments of 6th Bavarian Reserve Division between 26th Infantry Division and 3rd Bavarian Infantry Division, directing them to advance on a narrow front directly towards Wytschaete. Of priority importance, however, was the drive on Messines, so a huge effort was made to move the heavy artillery and adequate quantities of ammunition into position to provide fire support for a major assault on Messines the following day.

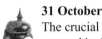

Gough's 2nd Division had a line of three and half miles to defend, for which he had a total of 3,250 rifles. His own division was only able to contribute 1,350 of these, the bulk of the rest coming from the London Scottish, along with supporting Indian Army infantry – the 57th and 129th – and 18/Hussars. One most helpful asset was the deployment of six batteries of French field artillery, supplementing his own three batteries of RHA.

As at Messines, heavy shelling commenced early, in this case at 6 am; but there was no significant attack that morning. The biggest threat came to the canal bridge to the north of Hollebeke, which had not been destroyed for lack of explosives. The German advance here was halted by fire from 4/Hussars, firing in enfilade from Hollebeke Wood.

Generalmajor Ritter von Clauss, Commander 6 Bavarian Infantry Brigade, whose command included Bavarian Infantry Regiment 17.

A projected attack by 4 Brigade and the newly deployed London Scottish at noon to assist in the defence of Messines failed to materialise – there were not sufficient troops and matters around Wytschaete itself mitigated against it. Gough's left was also substantially reinforced during the day – a French cavalry brigade came up by the canal, soon to be followed by four infantry battalions. Gough was able to withdraw 3 Brigade into reserve, whilst further reinforcements, in the shape of the French 9th Cavalry Division, also came up on the left.

A German attack against the London Scottish and 4 Brigade, as noted above, took place at about 4.45 pm; it lasted about forty five minutes but got nowhere. From 6.30 pm, Gough was able to reorganise his line; a further German attack took place at about 10.15 pm, but was beaten off. The Division, the *OH* records, had lost about thirty percent of the troops engaged in the four days 28 – 31 October.

31 October: The Right of I Corps

The crucial fighting in and around Gheluvelt, particularly on this day, is covered in the *Menin Road* volume of this trilogy, but it is as well to bear in mind that it was not just the Messines – Wytschaete Ridge that witnessed heavy fighting on 31 October. XV Corps, also a part of Army Group Fabeck, was equally intensively engaged and it is important to remember that none of these actions took place in isolation. Generalleutnant von Altrock, commanding 60 Infantry Brigade and deployed adjacent to the Ypres – Menin road, writing of the events of the day stated:

> On the orders of 30th Infantry Division, Oberstleutnant von Oldershausen and Infantry Regiment 105, supported by their right hand neighbouring formation, were to capture Gheluvelt. General von Altrock was to support this attack by means of one of his own launched by Infantry Regiment 99 and one battalion of Infantry Regiment 136 to the west of the Werwicq – Gheluvelt road. On the morning of 31 October, preliminary artillery fire came down on Gheluvelt. The staff of 60 Infantry Brigade moved to occupy a small house to the west of Oude Kruiseke, whilst the four battalions (three from Infantry Regiment 99 and one from Infantry Regiment 136) were deployed against Gheluvelt.
>
> The assault was launched against Gheluvelt and, a short time later, came a report that the commander of Infantry Regiment 99 [Oberstleutnant Nollau], who was in overall command, had been seriously wounded. At that, General von Altrock and his staff went forward through heavy harassing fire as far as the southern edge of Gheluvelt, where the regimental commander lay severely wounded and where Major Rock [Commanding Officer 3rd Battalion] Infantry Regiment 99 had been killed. There were severe casualties on both sides, but Gheluvelt had been captured. That same night General von Altrock went in search of a command post for the following day, but everywhere had been shot to pieces. They were surrounded by all the grimness of the battlefield; everywhere lay wounded soldiers, British as well as German, together with dying cattle, who let out bellows of pain. The howl of shells passing overhead, coupled with the crack of small arms fire, provided the aural backdrop. Large numbers of stragglers and shirkers were rounded up.
>
> It was difficult on 1 November to determine the positions of the battalions because of all the small arms fire that was flying about. General von Altrock selected a small building, Granat-Haüschen [Shell Cottage], situated just west of Gheluvelt, as a brigade command post. It was located close behind the infantry firing line and protected by a fold in the ground. Here, throughout this and the following days, we were under constant heavy artillery fire. The roof was pierced constantly by shrapnel balls and it kept raining tiles.

French 75mm gun in action - note the recoil. The French deployed increasing resources to assist the British, including artillery such as this.

Such was the demand in Germany for news from the front during 1914 that families often responded to appeals from local newspapers to allow them to print personal letters they had received. One such, relating to the fighting at the end of October, was passed to the *Leipziger Volkszeitung* by the family of a soldier in Infantry Regiment 105. Because it was of general interest it was republished by the *Freiburger Zeitung* some weeks later. It certainly succeeds in providing a flavour of the low level infantry battles south of the Menin Road at that time.

> *After a march of several days duration, we heard the thunder of the guns on 31 October ... What we experienced that day was a more appalling scene of war than it is possible for the normal mortal to comprehend ... There was an eerie silence then suddenly a Hauptmann from the 99th on our left shouted across, 'Prepare to attack! The assault begins at 1.00 pm!' We shook our heads in disbelief, because, thus far, anybody raising his head above the edge of the sunken road would have had it shot off. However, we made ready and waited patiently.*
>
> *At 12.45 pm the same Hauptmann suddenly shouted, 'Rapid fire!' We looked up and there, one hundred to one hundred and fifty metres away, the clay-yellow forms of the British, wearing caps of the same colour, were pulling back to the village behind*

them. We gave them all we had. The Hauptmann himself fired and I could hardly load fast enough ... Suddenly came the call 'Stop!' Our comrades off to the right had followed up towards the enemy trenches and there was a chance that we might have hit them. At this point the drums beat for the attack, the trumpets blew and, from thousands of throats, came shouts of Hurra! Hurra! We rushed forward like a wild storm, despite the weight of our knapsacks, with bayonets fixed and hunted the British out of their trenches, where they had made themselves extremely comfortable.

Their trenches were well constructed and equipped. To eat and drink there was corned beef, ham, chocolate, brandy and wine and there were ample quantities of cigars and cigarettes. Most of them were located behind hedgerows and hawthorn bushes. They had excellent overhead cover and featured tables, chairs, woollen blankets and mattresses. They fired at us from these trenches until we were a mere thirty metres away, then they emerged with their hands up and ran towards us to surrender. Despite their raised hands a great many were nevertheless shot down, some of us could not stop ourselves. We took several hundred prisoners ... the British were better infantrymen than the French. Some had sixteen years' service and most of them eight ...

My nerves were on edge and my heart was beating so loud I could hear it, but I stormed on, one amongst a wild horde rushing forward. The enemy was firing from every building. By now the sections included men from all the different regiments and they were attacking every trench and every building. Together with five other men, I overran three British supply waggons. Two men were attempting to guard them. Despite our charge, they would not yield, so we shot them down. We had a quick look in the waggons and found that they contained ammunition, rations and mail – most of which had been posted in London on 22 October.

This wing of I Corps, from Gheluvelt to the Comines Canal, was defended by Major General Bulfin's force and the remnants of Capper's 7th Division. The line was on the forward slope of the three spurs (marked by Tower Hamlets – a kilometre west of Gheluvelt, Shrewsbury Forest and Klein Zillebeke) that led down to Zandvoorde. Because these slopes were all wooded, the Germans did not have good observation of the British positions, which was probably just as well, as the defences were very thin.

See maps pp. 55 and 94

The plan for the day, following Haig's orders of the previous evening, were for the five battalions of French troops and accompanying

Zandvoorde Church.

The Earl of Cavan.

artillery under General Moussy, with their left on the canal, and Lord Cavan's and Bulfin's six battalions, to counter attack and recapture Hollebeke Chateau and Zandvoorde. The operation was to begin at 6.30 am and was to be supported by the artillery of 7th Division and some of the Cavalry Corps. In fact only three of the French battalions were available; these attacked according to the schedule but could only get forward about 300 yards and were forced to dig in, having come under sustained enfilade fire from south of the canal. Bulfin's force, who were to follow up, were prevented from doing so by the halting of the French advance; in any case a German bombardment opened up at 8 am, stopping any prospect of a counter attack.

7th Division was by now but a shadow of its former self; 22 Brigade was on the right (1/S/Staffs and 2/Warwicks in the line, 2/Queen's in support) and 21 Brigade on the left (2/Beds in the line, 2/GH in support). 20 Brigade was in reserve, east of Zillebeke. In fact much of the reserve during the night was deployed to dig trenches behind the left of 7th Division's position, which left 1/Grenadiers as the reserve in Herenthage Chateau – a princely total of eighty men.

By 10 am the German shelling had destroyed many of the British trenches – so effectively, indeed, that 2/Sussex were forced to withdraw into woods behind their position. The shelling continued mercilessly until 12.25 pm, when the Germany infantry commenced their attack in strength, substantially later than the move against Gheluvelt. The 7th Division was immediately in trouble on both its flanks.

The situation to the north was most desperate. The troops closest to the Menin Road had been swept away by 1 pm, as far south as the positions of 2/RSF and 2/Bedfords, astride the Zandvoorde-Gheluvelt road. However, the troops to the rear, including the Green Howards, were able to hold the Germans at bay and wrought considerable havoc. Nevertheless, the threat remained of an unravelling of the line from the north. 2/Warwicks were warned to provide left flank cover, but the men of 22 Brigade were now under enfilade fire and began to give way. Rallied by senior commanders, the brigade was led forward again at about 1.45 pm and the reserve of eighty men from 1/Grenadiers was brought up – although thirty of them became casualties in the approach.

Edward Bulfin,

Things became very confused. By 1.20 pm Major General Bulfin had been informed that 3 Brigade had fallen back from Gheluvelt and that 22 Brigade's left flank had collapsed. He gathered three of his battalion COs - 2/Sussex, 1/Northants and 2/Gordons - to work out a withdrawal. The risk of 2/Sussex being taken in rear if they did not get back was obvious, as lines of German infantry could be seen advancing on the left. He ordered his command to pivot back from the left, keeping contact with Lord Cavan's force on the right, forming a new line from Groenenberg Farm northwards to a track leading up to Hooge. This was desperate stuff.

The move began at 1.45 pm – just when 22 Brigade was moved forward again. The confusion led to the junction between Bulfin's force and 7th Division to weaken once more and give way, with men drifting off into Shrewsbury Forest. Bulfin instructed the Northamptons to stand fast in the wood on his right and ordered back 2/Gordons and half 2/Sussex to prepare a new position to the rear whilst, from his reserve, two companies of 2/Ox & Bucks were to take up position on Lord Cavan's left.

Thompson Capper.

Germans had already begun to infiltrate the British line. At 3 pm Capper issued a warning order to his division about the possibility of a withdrawal

93

Situation evening of 31 October NE of Hollebeke.

to a new line, Klein Zillebeke to Frezenberg, which had been envisioned in an instruction by Haig at 1.30 pm. The retreat had become such that the artillery on occasion found itself either in the firing line with the infantry or, in one instance, with the guns actually ahead of the infantry. In the midst of all this, the progress of the German advance had slowed, possibly because a significant number of officers had been killed. Bulfin decided on a counter attack and ordered 2/Gordons forward. He informed 2/Sussex and 1/Northamptons of the attack and instructed them to open fire as quickly as possible, 'the mad minute', when they heard cheering behind them.

The anticipated reinforcement of 200 men actually consisted of eighty. Still, they did as instructed, setting off with a yell and the Sussex and Northamptons duly opened up and then joined in with the charge; when the charge came level with the Ox & Bucks they, too joined in and, not to be outdone, 5/DG – also brought up to reinforce the line – added their weight on the left. Colonel Jeudwine, of Haig's staff and who had been in discussions with Bulfin at various stages during the crisis, reported the situation as he had left it to Haig near Hooge Chateau at about 4 pm. 6 (Cavalry) Brigade was ordered to the left of Cavan's position and was guided there by Jeudwine – hence the appearance of the Royals, with the 10th Hussars and the Northumberland Hussars in support.

The counter attack had the desired effect; not only was Bulfin's front stabilised but it also halted the German attack to the north, across 7th

Division's front. A general forward movement followed and a lot of ground that had been lost was recovered. Isolated pockets of resistance were dealt with – thus machine guns in houses overlooking the line were removed by bringing a gun up very close to the line and shelling them out. A wood south east of Shrewsbury Forest was strongly held and it took two organised attacks to clear it.

By 5.30 pm it was dark and Bulfin decided that it was necessary to call a halt to any further attempts to advance and to consolidate. The new 7th Division line ran from Herenthage Wood, with 20 Brigade on the left, 21 on the right and 22 in reserve; it then met Bulfin's force, holding the eastern and southern sides of Shrewsbury Forest, with the Ox & Bucks providing the connection with Cavan's force. Sorting out the men in the dark, in woodland, and digging in to new positions when exhausted would have tried fresh men sorely; but it was done and even rations and water were got forward.

The *OH* states that the three brigades of the 7th Division were considerably reduced by the end of 31 October – 20 Brigade was down to 940 men, with each battalion having only five officers; 21 Brigade had 750 men and 22 Brigade probably fewer than 800. 2/Sussex, in Bulfin's force, suffered 405 casualties on 30 and 31 October. It is worth noting that during the fighting around Ypres in 1914 the British did receive reinforcements – for example, a few days later the total number of rifles available in 7th Division had increased considerably, albeit from a very low starting point.

The conclusion that was reached by the Germans at the end of what must have been a disappointing day for them was to continue the pressure on Messines Ridge. However, to avoid heavy casualties from British fire it was decided that a night operation would be risked.

1 November: Attacks at Wytschaete and the fall of Messines
The early hours of 1 November saw continuous shelling of the buildings along the ridge, the gunners aided by bright moonlight. The severe action this day commenced on that part of the ridge dominated by Wytschaete. It has already been noted that the battle for Messines was an extremely hard proposition, even for the experienced and battle-hardened Württembergers of 26th Infantry Division. Just to their north 6th Bavarian Reserve Division, which was as inexperienced as the reserve corps of Duke Albrecht's Fourth Army, faced almost insurmountable problems. Their first attempt to capture Wytschaete failed completely. About mid afternoon on 31 October Bavarian Reserve Infantry Regiment 21 was ordered to advance to the Wambeke area east of the Warneton – Oosttaverne road, there to be subordinated to 12

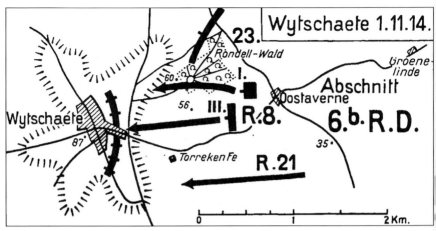

The assault on Wytschaete 1 November.

Bavarian Reserve Brigade and to prepare to launch a night attack against Wytschaete. To state that this was a tall order is barely to hint at the difficulties they faced. Barely more than month earlier the men had been undergoing basic platoon level training, now they were being called on to conduct an attack in the dark and across unknown terrain against an enemy of unknown strength and dispositions. This would have been a considerable gamble and a challenge for any active army unit; it was simply expecting too much of such an inexperienced formation.

The situation was just as problematic for the equally inexperienced

An artist's impression of the assault on Wytschaete.

gunners of Bavarian Reserve Field Artillery Regiment 6. They had been providing fire support to the west of Hollebeke, but now had to concentrate on Wytschaete. One of the gunners, Kriegsfreiwilliger Schuster, described some of the difficulties they encountered, underlining the operational problems.

About 5.00 pm on the evening of 31 October, we arrived in Houthem, which was ablaze. Only with difficulty could we get the horses to move forward in amongst all the smoke and flames of the burning houses. The battle had also left its mark outside the village, where medical orderlies were busy tending to the wounded and gathering together the fallen. The fields and ditches were littered with abandoned equipment and shell baskets. Darkness was already falling when the battery went into position in a field surrounded by hedges not far from Kaleute. The gunners then set to, to dig in the guns and ammunition waggons. As far as the falling light permitted, the ground out to the front was observed; in the west this was crowned by a low hill feature. Upon it were situated Wytschaete, with Messines on fire to the south.

By now it was dark, so the flash of guns firing, the explosions of enemy shells and the sight of burning farms in all directions made a striking, if sad, impression. We did manage to grab a quick meal from the insulated containers; it was the first warm food of the day. It was about 9.00 pm when we opened fire on Wytschaete. The moment when the order 'Fire!' was given was an unforgettable occasion. It was not until midnight that the loud sound of battle began to die away. Wytschaete was a sea of flames and the church tower first tilted and then collapsed. It was now All Saints' Day. For many this religious holiday was also to be their last day! We were manning our guns at 2.00 am when we were ordered to change positions forward.

In near silence the teams arrived and we moved along a field track at a walk. Because it was narrow and the infantry were also marching forward along it, we had to halt frequently. Finally we arrived at Oosttaverne and three guns of the battery went into position at its western exit. [Our] fourth gun, commanded by Offizierstellvertreter Jaenisch, was sent forward, together with an ammunition waggon, along the road to Wytschaete, so as to accompany the forward troops of Bavarian Reserve Infantry Regiment 17. The gun soon bore off to the left along a track that petered out and we were reduced to carrying on cross country

See map
p. 96

97

*until we unharnessed behind a hedge. The gun was run forward
to a point about one hundred metres from a lone house and
ammunition was moved forward. The team remained in cover
behind the hedge.*

*All around it was relatively quiet, though now and again we
heard rifle or machine gun fire. We were in an odd sort of position,
because we had no contact with the infantry. We aimed at
Wytschaete and opened fire. We had barely fired one shell than a
hail of small arms fire came from the right. Some flew overhead,
the rest rattled against the gun shield. We threw ourselves to the
ground and took up our carbines, ready to shoot. The shots came
from Rondell Wood [on British maps, Oosttaverne Wood] about
one hundred and fifty metres away. There was enemy in the wood
and we had passed through our own lines in the darkness. The
first thing, therefore, was to withdraw our gun so that we should
not be caught out. Under a torrent of fire, which fortunately passed
overhead, we hauled the gun and as much ammunition as possible
back behind the hedge, but we had to leave the ammunition wagon
where it was. We remained behind the hedge, ready to fire to cover
the withdrawal of the gun then, when we thought that it was back
in safety, we pulled back ourselves, moving in bounds until we
were safely back with the battery. The wagon was recovered the
following day.*

At 10.00 pm Bavarian Reserve Infantry Regiment 17, then deployed in
contact in a wooded area west of Hollebeke, was also ordered to
participate in the attack on Wytschaete. This involved an awkward move
at night to be on their start line, approximately three hundred metres from
the first British outposts by 1.00 am. The fact that this was achieved was
a feather in their caps; it would have taxed a fully trained unit. Lined up
to the right of Infantry Regiment 122, the attack began promptly at 2.00
am. However, that was when the difficulties began. The advance was over
unrecconoitred and unknown terrain, which was littered with all manner
of obstacles to movement: thick hedges running in unfavourable
directions, deep and wide ditches, boggy areas and so on. Small wonder,
therefore, that coordinated movement and maintenance of direction was
almost impossible. Had the British defence been stronger it is most
improbable that the attackers would have entered Wytschaete or even
gained a foothold on the ridge.

Against the odds, however, the Bavarians did manage to begin to
fight forward into the village, but then an entirely self-made disaster
unfolded. Yet again the expedient of issuing forage caps to the regiments

of 6th Bavarian Reserve Division turned out to be a self-inflicted wound on a large scale. In the half light of early dawn, men from Bavarian Reserve Infantry Regiment 21, who were advancing on Wytschaete from the east, assumed wrongly that they were observing British troops to their front. There then occurred what was described as, 'a battle with many casualties ... until it was ended with considerable difficulty by the intervention of individual officers'. If proof were needed of the folly of deploying these units over hastily and with inadequate preparation, this nonsensical event provides it.

By about 4.30 am, Bavarian Reserve Infantry Regiment 17, which had got into the eastern part of Wytschaete and was consolidating its hold on the place, suddenly found itself the victims of the serious friendly fire incident. There was of course no means of direct See map p. 87 communication between the regiments, so it was most unfortunate that neither had any idea about the precise location of the other. Bavarian Reserve Infantry Regiment 17 stated subsequently:

> *Towards 5.00 am, elements of Bavarian Reserve Infantry Regiment 21 launched an attack on Wytschaete from the east near Torreken Farm. Despite the waving of flags and unfurling the regimental colour, notwithstanding the giving of German signals and the singing of 'Die Wacht am Rhein', it was impossible to correct the error. Our sister regiment charged in amongst us and wrecked the carefully created order. Only gradually did the officers restore order.*

As it became light, the surviving British sub-units in the area began a series of hasty counter attacks. These were supported directly by flanking units and artillery batteries to the rear and indirectly by German guns firing on the wrong targets or in the misapprehension that the village was still in British hands. This situation, on top of the previous chaos and subsequent losses, meant that Oberst Großmann of Bavarian Reserve Infantry Regiment 17 decided that, lacking fresh troops, he had no choice but to order a withdrawal. This duly occurred about mid morning. The Bavarians had come close to a local success but in pulling back to Wambeke they had in fact achieved nothing and had suffered casualties of almost thirty percent.

From the perspective of the British defenders, they noted that shelling of the village included the use of 210mm (8.3inch) howitzers. At 1 am on 1 November an infantry attack in considerable strength, approaching from the east and south east, commenced against Wytschaete, held by the Composite Household Cavalry Regiment of 4

Brigade with 415 men; and also the ridge between it and the windmill, defended by part of the London Scottish and 6/DG, with 294 and 300 rifles respectively.

Surgeon Major Cowie, of the Composite Regiment, noted of the events of 31 October and 1 November:

> *31 October – Regiment in the trenches east of Wytschaete, 1st Life Guards' Squadron on the right of the line, the machine gun holding the extreme of their flank at the cross roads to Messines (south) and Oosttaverne (east), the trenches running along the eastern or farther side of the St Eloi road. There were a few casualties in the evening – Trooper Lewry being killed* [commemorated on the Menin Gate], *Impleton and two others wounded. All day the high explosive shells were exploding over Wytschaete, especially directed at the wood north west* [Bois de Wytschate] *and the Kemmel road.*
>
> *Before midnight the enemy could be heard making a great noise on our left front, blowing horns, playing bands and shouting; they could be seen later passing across our front from the north east, and they fell upon our trenches held by the 1st Life Guards' Squadron. The enemy gained a footing here, but a counter attack was ordered and our men, who got into the trenches again, led by Lieutenant Leigh and Lieutenant Smith (Captain Wyndham being wounded) did some execution among the Germans, many of whom appeared very young. 1 November: The enemy, however, were in too great strength, and we fell back through Wytschaete in the direction of Kemmel. During this retirement, before we had got clear of Wytschaete, Major Lord Crichton* [buried at Zantvoorde Military Cemetery] *and Lieutenant Smith* [buried at Bedford House] *were lost, and Lieutenant Leigh was wounded Some of the Lincolns had come up in support in the early morning and helped to check the enemy's advance, which, however, was never pressed beyond the outskirts of Wytschaete in the Kemmel direction.*

In Wytschaete itself the Germans established themselves in the village by 2.45 am and the defenders were left hanging on to its western and southern edges, whilst to the north 20/Hussars (5 Brigade) remained in control. Attempts were then made to regain the village. The first attempt, by 12/Lancers, failed – in part because, in the darkness, they appear to have been fired at by both sides. A further attempt would have to await daylight.

Gough had ordered up two battalions of Shaw's 9 (Infantry) Brigade, sent north from Smith-Dorrien's II Corps, recently arrived at Kemmel, when the intensity of the attack on Wytschaete became apparent. When they got within 400 metres of the village they were combined with 3/Hussars and ordered to launch an immediate attack – 1/Lincolns in the fore with half of 1/Northumberland Fusiliers (1/NFus). This attack was beaten off, mainly by German fire but also because of confusion caused by the as yet dim light and by shouted orders to retire, possibly coming from the Germans. The attackers took cover in folds in the ground about 200 yards short of the position. An attack by two companies of the French 32nd Division, coming from the direction of Vierstraat, was also seen off. The British remained in these exposed positions, enfiladed as they became, to cover the withdrawal of the London Scottish and others from the ridge; and in due course were able to withdraw with surprisingly few casualties. Nevertheless, the Lincolns suffered eight officer and 293 other rank casualties – of the hundred or so killed, only See maps pp.75 and 109 six have a known grave – and the Fusiliers five officers and ninety three other ranks in the course of the action.

1/Lincolns had a torrid time of it. They had marched to Kemmel from Éstaires, via Neuve Eglise and Lindenhoek, starting at 6.45 am on the 31st, a march of twelve miles – although tiring, 'the relief from the dreadful trenches at Neuve Chapelle was very welcome', as the regimental history puts it. Orders were received from Gough at 1.30 am on 1 November: 'that the battalion was to march to Wytschaete and retake the trenches from which the cavalry had been driven'. The CO, Lieutenant Colonel WEB Smith, noted that this 'was obviously a difficult task, as it was dark and impossible to locate the trenches'. The counter attack had 3/Hussars and 1/Northumberland Fusiliers (NF) on the left.

The battalion deployed on the right of the Kemmel-Wytschaete road and advanced in two lines. On reaching a railway cutting on the south western side of the village they were fired on 'by people whom we thought to be native troops, as they called out several Hindustani words'. ... By now many had been killed and wounded, for the enemy had advanced a machine gun on the right of the cutting and was firing down into the congested ranks of the Lincolns. Both commanders of A and B Companies became casualties.

The battalion now fell back about a hundred yards, taking as many of the wounded as possible. Many deeds of gallantry occurred during this retirement. Meanwhile the Germans were rapidly entrenching themselves, singing and shouting.

101

On the arrival of the Northumberland Fusiliers on the left of the Lincolnshire, the latter were ordered by Brigadier General Shaw (commanding 9 Brigade, 3rd Division) *to push the attack. Colonel Smith then ordered his men to attack the railway cutting in front.*

It must have been somewhere near dawn when this most gallant attempt was made ... Under very heavy rifle fire and machine gun fire, the battalion rushed forward against the enemy who, in considerable strength, was by now strongly entrenched. Many fell dead and wounded, but still the Lincolnshire persevered in the attack and got to within a few yards of the German trenches. The survivors (for by now the battalion had suffered very heavy losses) took the only cover that they could get, a very tiny fold in the ground, about one hundred yards from the position so strongly held by the enemy.

Here the remnants of the battalion lay until about 6.45 am. Daylight disclosed their position and soon they were under merciless artillery fire from the enemy's guns as well as rifle fire from both flanks while, to make matters worse, their own gunners shelled them. From this terrible position it was imperative to withdraw, but how to do it! At great risk, Colonel Smith had only been able to keep in touch with the situation of his battalion by crawling from company to company and now he saw that the only thing to do was to make a dash for a hedgerow and small fold in the ground in rear. 'On Colonel Smith giving the word (war diary extract), we got up and ran for our lives towards the dip, the enemy opening a murderous fire but, probably owing to surprise and excitement, a great many of their shots went high and many of us succeeded in reaching shelter.'

The survivors formed a rough line; the next thing to cross on their retirement was a long, glacis like slope [leading up to the ridge on which Spanbroekmolen sat, that position being held by 3/Hussars]. *On emerging from cover, the battalion once again came under heavy fire, but fortunately suffered only a few casualties. At last the glacis slope was passed and the Lincolnshire, strung out into skirmishing order, fell back in the direction of Kemmel.*

The battalion, now numbering less that a hundred all ranks, reached the road near Kemmel and marched back in the direction of Lindenhoek, where on the eastern side of the village they were formed up by the Colonel and the Adjutant. 'Here [war diary] *we were joined by three Special reserve officers and about a hundred men who had managed to escape. At the time the battalion numbered 175.'*

A British artist's interpretation of the involvement of the London Scottish in the Battle of Messines. He even depicted the jamming of British rifles experienced during the fighting. © Taylor Library

Meanwhile, for the defenders on Messines Ridge the problem that night of 31 October/1 November was that they had no continuous line and the Germans were able to infiltrate through them. To return to the London Scottish, whom we saw had fended off a German attack at about midnight but then faced another onslaught at 2 am, 1 November

> *A great wave of shouting men with bayonets fixed surged in upon the London Scottish centre and left, poured over the advanced trenches and reached the road, forcing back the line by mere weight of numbers. The charge swept around the left flank, pushed in between it and the cavalry trenches, and getting through to the left rear interposed between the former line and the reserve on Enfer height. This was for the London Scottish the most critical moment of the battle. If the height were lost and the flank enveloped, nothing could save the battalion from destruction. Colonel Malcolm realised the danger. A charge of part of his small reserve pushed back the Bavarians who were working around the flank and, after a sharp fight, touch was regained with the left of the hard pressed line.*

On the extreme left part of C Company got cut off and threatened to be overrun; however, they managed to work their way northwards and then

103

north westwards. Dependent on the moon for direction – no map – they eventually found themselves close to Vierstraat at about dawn, having managed to get past Wytschaete without bumping into either friend or foe.

Back on the ridge,

It now became a prolonged and confused struggle, in which the irregular line swayed backwards and forwards, the enemy breaking in here and there, and being met and pushed back again by local counter attacks of little groups of men. There was hard fighting, bayonets were crossed, fire was exchanged at close quarters. Officers, sergeants and men had to act on their own initiative. There was no communication with brigade headquarters and no knowledge of what was happening on the rest of the line. The London Scottish simply fought doggedly to hold their ground against the mass of enemies that was trying to force them back. Losses were heavy. Several of the officers had been wounded, and Captain MacNab, the Medical Officer, had been killed in the first rush, bayoneted whilst helping a wounded man. ...

At last Colonel Malcolm decided that if what was left of the battalion was not to be enveloped and destroyed he must extricate it from its perilous position. ... He directed a retirement across the Steenbeck valley towards Wulverghem. Gradually the various detachments that were strung out along the slope of the ridge were disengaged and drew together as they fell back. Companies had been reduced to the strength of sections. Many of those still in the ranks were wounded. Other wounded men straggled back, assisted by comrades in nearly as bad a plight as themselves. All were weary and exhausted with the unequal struggle.

The roll call near Wolverghem after the Battle of Messines. Only 150 officers and men answered. In the days that followed stragglers turned up and finally it was determined that 394 officers and men had been killed or were missing. © Taylor Library

Amongst these wounded was Ronald Coleman, the misfortune probably saving him for what turned out to be a stellar career in Hollywood. Suffering from a shattered ankle, he was discharged as medically unfit six months later. Eighty five men are listed as killed by the CWGC for the period 31 October - 2 November – and only two of these have a known grave, in Wytschaete Military Cemetery. The battalion was actually deployed again on the same day. 18/Hussars were moved forward to hold a line forward and to the south of Spanbroekmolen, which overlooked the valley between it and Messines Ridge. It was part of the last ridge line between Messines and Kemmel. The London Scottish, with stragglers from other regiments, held the line on the Wulverghem road; in the afternoon, with no further concerted action by the Germans and with reinforcements coming up, the London Scottish were able to withdraw to Kemmel (where Sir John French happened to be that afternoon). In the action at Messines the regiment had lost 394 all ranks. However, as we have seen, in Wytschaete what had looked so promising for the Germans gradually turned into dust. At 8 am 20/Hussars, with assistance from 12/Lancers, broke into the north of the village; combined with a more determined push from the French 32nd Division, the result was that the Germans were, at least temporarily, cleared out of Wytschaete. The arrival of the French, who during the day took over all of the line from east of the Comines Canal to Wytschaete and beyond to its south west, was extremely timely. It meant that 2nd (Cavalry) Division could be withdrawn from the line – 3 Brigade to Spanbroekmolen, 5 Brigade to Kemmel and 4 Brigade to Westoutre, whilst its associated infantry concentrated at Locre. The Germans managed once more to force an entry into the eastern part of the village at 4 pm, but only for a short time before they were once again cleared out.

Kriegsfreiwilliger Ludwig Engstler, a soldier with 4th Company Bavarian Reserve Infantry Regiment 17, who was one of those on the receiving end of the friendly fire incident and who was slightly wounded, described the attack in a letter written whilst he was recovering in hospital. Although he did not allude directly to the error made by Bavarian Reserve Infantry Regiment 21, he did provide a vivid description of the chaotic nature of the battle that very sanguinary day.

> *Do not be shocked, in two days' time I shall be back in action. I have a bayonet wound in my right thigh. I have headed this letter 'All Souls' Day'* [2 November]. *My God, the words 'All Souls' conceal a tremendous amount. Let me explain it to you. During the evening of 31 October the Oberst said to us, 'Comrades. It all begins today! His Majesty the Kaiser himself has ordered that the*

village of Wytschaete is to be stormed and held. Both the Kaiser and the Crown Prince [Rupprecht] *will be observing the battle. Act like brave Bavarians!' We moved forward joyfully; it was still night when were arrived at our place of battle. The guns were already making a tremendous racket. Everywhere the shells groaned their way to the horizon. The German artillery was the stronger and did not grant the enemy any sort of breathing space. We shook out and launched into battle.*

At that everything opened up on us: guns, machine guns and rifle fire. Our ranks began to thin, as here and there our comrades fell. However the unholy howling and rushing sounds of the shells did not throw us off balance. Forwards! Not a step backwards! It was 12 o'clock midnight. 'Fix bayonets!' We closed our ranks in tightly and went forward like a wall of flashes. Every gap which appeared in the wall was rapidly filled. With shouts of Hurra! we pushed on into the village. From all sides a raging rate of fire was poured at us from within the houses. We set fire to them and the flames blazed upwards, illuminating a grim scene. The streets were full of dead and wounded men: dark skinned Indians, together with British, French and Belgians [sic. presumably local inhabitants], *all lying alongside rows of our courageous Bavarians. We drove the British out of the village, which now belonged to us. The British, however, summoned reinforcements and pushed forward. We came under fire from the entrances to cellars and every other nook and cranny.*

There were too few of us. There were no officers in sight and we just had to pull back. Once more we advanced and once more we retreated. It was a saddened platoon which turned its back on this place of death. 'Are you still alive?' asked one of the few who remained. It seemed to me that I had been granted new life; something which was permitted to very few. I cried with anger when I saw all the misery around me. A man ran past me. I glanced at him and saw that it was Jordan Mattias. Deeply moved, we shook hands in silence. On All Saints Day [1 November] *there was a regimental roll call. More than half the regiment was missing. The other regiments who had also fought on this day suffered equally dreadful losses. Today is All Souls Day, when the living remember the dead. However, we are proud that we were present during a great battle, which worked out in our favour* [sic.] *and which the Kaiser and the Crown Prince witnessed. Within two to three days nothing more will be heard about the British troops but this* [for us] *was less a baptism of fire and more a baptism in blood.*

106

How did I come to be wounded? We were in the village and pursuing the enemy when, suddenly, I felt something sharp and metallic pierce my thigh. I threw my leg forward quickly, so that it did not penetrate far, then I went back to my opponent. It was a wounded British soldier, who was aiming his rifle at me. His instrument of death flew into the mire and I despatched him to Hell with one thrust. Then we pushed on. It was not until after the roll call that I had my wound dressed and I have now been in hospital for nearly two days. I shall then be out just in time to take part in the decisive battle. May God protect me as he has thus far.

What did I experience during the battle? I was relieved that it had finally got going. The never ending marching was not at all to my liking. The first time shrapnel burst over us, we all ducked down low, but we soon got used to it. I was very lucky during the assault. Men were falling to my front, my right and my left, but I remained on my feet. I gave up all hope of surviving and, in this fatalistic mood, did not seek cover, but moved around upright. I shall have to stitch up two holes in my clothes caused by these damned British soldiers. In the village we came up against a mixed group of twenty British and Indian troops. There were about twelve of us and we opened fire at once.

The Hauptmann was stationed at the entrance to the village and called for volunteers to go and collect the wounded and bring them into the shelter of the undamaged buildings. I volunteered for this rather risky task. We carried about two dozen into two houses and made them comfortable. All of a sudden there was firing on all sides. Some of our comrades raced by and shouted to us, 'The British are coming!' We had to pull back. We took the slightly wounded men with us, but we had to leave the others behind. We could not remain there; we realised that it was pointless to stay and be killed, so off we went! I took the arm of my Leutnant and supported him, but suddenly he was shot through the temples and fell dead, so I went and joined the others. A word about the battle in general. It was one of the largest to date. The British were attacked all along the front and suffered similar casualties to us. They were hemmed in a horseshoe-like position and could not get away. You will be able to read more about it in the papers. Most of our officers have fallen.

Of course this attack was anything but a German success. Its failure can be easily explained. It was carried out by men who had received very little training and who had to advance over difficult and unknown terrain in the dark. To that must be added a serious friendly fire incident and misdirected German artillery fire. Possibly better trained units would have had more success, but it would still have been a difficult operation in testing circumstances. Apart from any other consideration, because the German units off to the north could not advance beyond Oosttaverne Woods, it would still have been necessary to split the regiment to provide flank protection to the right, thus weakening the overall attack on Wytschaete itself. In the event, this first attempt on Wytschaete caused the regiment casualties of more than thirty per cent, including these officers, all killed in action: Major Hermann Helmes, commanding officer 2nd Battalion, Hauptmann Georg Danner and Landwehr Oberleutnant Theodor Harster, commanders of 3rd and 6th Companies respectively, together with Leutnants Georg Fillweber, Anton Halder, Michael Sacherl and Rudolf Schuster. During the following days, on 4 November in particular, the regiment lost a further twelve officers killed in action, so by the time the regiment was relieved Engstler's statement accurately summarised the situation. Subsequent battlefield clearance meant that all these officers have known graves. Most lie in the Kamaradengrab at Langemarck, but two are buried in the cemetery at Menen.

Messines, apart from persistent shelling during the night, was a relatively calmer spot during the early morning of 1 November. Allenby had given permission for the village itself to be evacuated, so long as the ridge beyond was secured but, as has been mentioned, it took a determined push by the German army finally to clear through the built up area. Once it became clear that 4 Brigade had been driven off the ridge to the north, de Lisle ordered his men to fall back, covered by the London Scottish, to Wulverghem Ridge, to the south of Spanbroekmolen.

See map p. 109

South of Messines, 4th Division ordered the Inniskilling Fusiliers to withdraw to the south of the Douve and to place their left flank parallel with it; a squadron of 19th Hussars was used to fill the gap between them and the right of 1st Division. However, the message failed to get through to two companies, who remained in position in their shallow, wet trenches. Further south, 4th Division held off attacks against the front north of the Lys, in particular the defences of Ploegsteert Wood. An attempt by the Germans to secure Douve Farm, which was not actually held permanently by the British, broke down because the two isolated companies were able to bring down effective fire whilst the German artillery seemed to be unable to locate them accurately.

In the midst of this raging battle, one member of Bavarian Reserve Infantry Regiment 17 had an astonishing experience. On 12 November

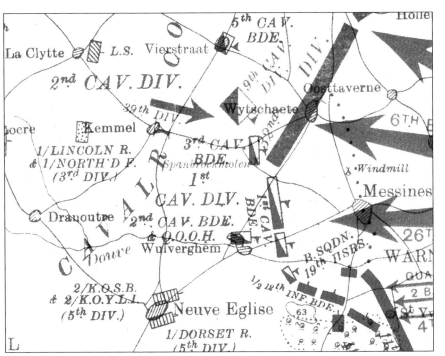

Situation on Messines Ridge 1 November.

the Corps Commander, General der Infanterie Karl Ritter von Martini, wrote to Headquarters Sixth Army to describe what happened.

I wish to draw your attention to the following extraordinary action:

During the night 31 October/1 November 3rd Company Bavarian Reserve Infantry Regiment 17 became split up during bitter house to house fighting in Wytschaete. Only a few men reached the edge of the village with the company commander and all but one [of these] were killed in the [subsequent] fire fight. The only survivor was Infanterist Johann Zott, whose knapsack was holed by shell splinters. Zott disguised himself in the coat and cap of a dead British soldier, who was lying next to him. He then ran to a position behind the line of British riflemen and went up to where the ammunition wagons and field kitchens were located. He remained there for several hours, drank some coffee with the British soldiers, busied himself around an ammunition wagon and fed the horses.

As dawn approached, Zott feared that he would be unmasked, so he mounted the saddle horse, drove the wagon forward to the

British firing line and emptied the ammunition. It came in useful that Zott, a former seaman, knew a number of English expressions and swear words. Whilst the British soldiers were occupied with the ammunition, Zott mounted suddenly and galloped off past the trenches in the direction of the German lines, under heavy fire from both sides. Luckily he found cover in a small hollow. Here he was able to swap his British clothing for German, because there were dead and wounded German soldiers in the hollow. Once he had loaded a wounded officer and three wounded soldiers on his wagon, he drove on towards the German position. Towards evening he arrived at Headquarters II Bavarian Army Corps with his wagon and three wounded men – the officer had died on the journey. I have awarded the man, who is a Kriegsfreiwilliger from Augsburg, the Iron Cross Second Class.

 By the morning of **2 November** the French held five miles of the front south of Ypres – from north east of the Comines Canal to Spanbroekmolen. The last part of 2nd (Cavalry) Division in the front, 3 Brigade, was replaced by French cavalry early in the morning and the division was now in reserve. General d'Urbal, who on 20 October had been appointed commander of the French forces in the north (Le Détachement d'Armée de Belgique, or DAB for convenience), instructed his troops to recapture the ground between the Douve and Messines, retake Messines itself and for the forces in Wytschaete to push forward in the direction of Houtem, the whole to commence at about 10 am.

However, the Germans had other ideas, for they placed their emphasis for attacks on this day on the Wytschaete sector – and their attack started first, at approximately 8.30 am. The consequence was that the French were driven out of the village – although hanging on to positions to the north west, in Wytschaete Wood; whilst the line near the canal also threatened to buckle, though it was stabilised by about 5 pm. The 1st (Cavalry) Division, on the right of the French, assisted the French as possible but, apart from being severely shelled in the morning, did not take part in any assault apart from lending the French the use of its artillery. 4th Division, to the right, continued to feel considerable German pressure and was reinforced by the placing of two rather weak battalions under its command.

 Obviously the failure by the Germans to take and hold Wytschaete on 1 November did not spell the end of operations on this part of Messines Ridge. Well before Bavarian Reserve Infantry Regiment 17 was forced to pull back from the village, 6th Bavarian Reserve Division had already decided to reinforce the front and renew the attack with fresh forces on 2 November. This decision was recorded word for word in the war diary.

7.00 am. Enemy in Wytschaete once more. From 12 [Bavarian] *Reserve Brigade.* [Bavarian] *Reserve Infantry Regiment 17 is 500 metres east of the built up area;* Bavarian] *Reserve Infantry Regiment 21 is on the adjoining hill to the south. In order to speed up the capture of the enemy strong point Wytschaete, another two battalions of* [Bavarian] *Reserve Infantry Regiment 8 have been released from Corps reserve and have been placed at our disposal. Admittedly this is because it was thought a breakthrough in this area might have been possible. The allocation was, however, urgently needed because* [Bavarian] *Reserve Infantry Regiment 17 needed a break, so Commander 12* [Bavarian] *Reserve Brigade has received fresh troops.*

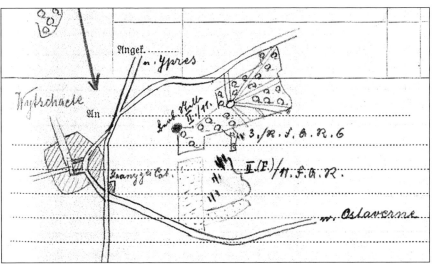

Gun positions east of Wytschaete on 2 November.

Oberleutnant Herbert Wurmb, Adjutant Bavarian Reserve Infantry Regiment 8, who later became well known as the officer who led the recapture of the Schwaben Redoubt near Thiepval on 1 July 1916, described what happened next:

It was on All Saints' Day 1914, a beautiful Sunday in autumn, that troops of 6th Bavarian Reserve Division captured Wytschaete but, due to several unfortunate circumstances, the village had to be

111

Oberst Hartmann, Commander Bavarian Reserve Infantry Regiment 8, at Wytschaete in November.

completely evacuated once more. However, the divisional commander, [General der Kavallerie] *Freiherr von Speidel, did not regard the battle as lost.* [Bavarian] *Reserve Infantry Regiment 20 and our regiment, less 2nd Battalion ... was given the mission of renewing the attack at 2.00 pm. The regimental commander, Oberst Hartmann, and I, as regimental adjutant, were despatched in advance to Groenelinde* [Linde], *where we were met by the commander of 12 Reserve Brigade, General*[major] *Kiefhaber. He issued orders for the assault on Wytschaete. The 1st Battalion* [Hauptmann Oskar Prager] *and 3rd Battalion* [Major Oskar Bezzel] *advanced as far as Oosttaverne, where they halted, because it was not known whether the enemy or we were occupying Wytschaete. From here, 3rd Battalion pushed forward patrols towards Wytschaete.*

The artillery preparation of the attack was provided by the heavy artillery of 6th Bavarian Reserve Division [Reserve Foot Artillery Battalion 6] *and 3rd Division. The light field howitzers of Bavarian Reserve Field Artillery Regiment 6 were also involved, but the field guns were distributed as infantry support batteries amongst the two brigades of 6th Bavarian Reserve Division and located in the front line. In accordance with the mission, the 3rd Battalion, together with Reserve Infantry Regiment 17, was to assault and capture Wytschaete. To the northeast of Wytschaete, it was to link up with Bavarian Infantry Regiment 23 at the Rondellwald [British Oostaverne Wood], whilst its left flank was to move along the line of the Oostaverne – Wytschaete road, maintaining contact with Bavarian Reserve Infantry Regiment 21. 1st Battalion was to follow up echeloned to the right.*

The attack began at 1.45 pm. Zeitler's battery kept up a constant fire on Wytschaete, lifting only when 3rd Battalion began to advance, in the face of very heavy small arms fire from Rondellwald. There was a gap of about two kilometres with the 3rd Division until that evening, when a battalion from that division had closed it. As a result Major Bezzel requested the Regiment to deploy 1st Battalion in his support. At that a platoon of 2nd Company was sent forward and established that the southern edge of this wood was free of enemy forces and pushed on further to the western edge. Initially this did not make much of a difference to 3rd Battalion but, at 2.30 pm, a further attempt was made by the entire company to clear the wood. Meanwhile Reserve Infantry Regiment 17 was withdrawn completely from the firing line, having suffered insupportable casualties.

About 2.00 pm the 3rd Battalion was occupying reasonable cover in a hollow some 800 metres east of Wytschaete. Enemy shelling was having no effect. Grehn's patrol from 10th Company reported, 'Southern sector of Wytschaete is free of enemy, but there are strong groups of enemy in the northern part'. Towards 3.00 pm Major Bezzel ordered an attack on Wytschaete. In order to reduce the risk of casualties, the men were ordered to spread out and to advance individually as far as a fold in the ground a few hundred metres from the eastern edge of Wytschaete and to form up there. Reserve Leutnant Graser, commanding 10th Company, received a head wound and was replaced by Reserve Leutnant Schaurer. Major Bezzel hurried forward with his adjutant, Oberleutnant Bärmann (Infantry Regiment 4) and 10th Company, to the track running from Oosttaverne – Wytschaete, passing racks of drying tobacco and under extremely heavy flanking fire.

There was a short breather in the hollow from where it was possible to observe troops, apparently from Bavarian Reserve Infantry Regiment 21, advancing and then digging in at the southern end of Wytschaete. Once more Major Bezzel repeated his orders for the assault on the village and directed that there be no halt until the western edge was reached. Rushing out in front himself and not far from the houses began he came under fire from a rough brushwood shelter and suddenly felt a heavy blow on the thigh – wounded! He made his way back into the first house he came across, which happened to be on fire, made it his command post and his wound was tended by Infanterist Pfirsching of 10th Company... Leutnants Böck [11th] *and* Mantel [officer commanding 12th] *were also wounded and Offizierstellvertreter Hacker, a platoon commander in 9th Company, was killed.*

The adjutant 3rd Battalion [Oberleutnant Heinrich Bärmann] *observed the progress of the battle from the roof of the command post. 9th Company had formed a front facing the enemy in the Rondellwald whilst, to the left, 10th Company appeared to have deployed. Then, once 2nd and 4th Companies had opened fire just before 4.00 pm on the groups of houses and pockets of resistance from the western edge of the Rondellwald, 3rd Battalion* [primarily 9th and 10th Companies] *supported by 3rd Company, which advanced to the south of Rondellwald in contact with 3rd Battalion, pressed the attack against the eastern edge of the village and succeeded in capturing a line of enemy trenches by about 5.30 pm. Two light enemy machine guns, which the 3rd Battalion captured and which were placed that evening in a house east of the village, were unfortunately moved to the rear the following day by Bavarian Infantry Regiment 22.*

There was an unfortunate occurrence at 5.20 pm when our own artillery brought fire down once more on the village. Our 10th Company, which had already pressed on into the village, received heavy casualties as a result. Despite every effort by the commanding officer of 3rd Battalion, waving with artillery flags, towels and coats, the artillery continued to fire and to damage 10th Company, such that it had to withdraw. Once the small arms fire from the flank had slackened, Major Bezzel, supported by Infanterist Pfirsching and leaning on his sword, hobbled back to Oosttaverne, whence he was transported back to the homeland. Oberleutnant Bärmann assumed command of 3rd Battalion that evening. He and Leutnant Fritsching, officer commanding 9th Company, were the only officers of the battalion still on their feet.

Bärmann amalgamated the 9th and 11th Companies into one, Feldwebel Eberling commanded the 10th and Feldwebel Mayer the 12th...

During the night the troops dug in, together with the grenade launcher teams. In accordance with divisional orders the village perimeter was to be held at all costs. Many of the wounded were evacuated, but it was a difficult operation. The shadows darkened and night fell, heavy and serious, on the bloody Sunday that was All Saints' Day 1914, the weapons fell silent and the fallen took their rest.

Panoramic sketch of Messines by an OP of Field Artillery Regiment 29, 26th Infantry Division, 2 November.

The War Diary of 6th Bavarian Reserve Division for that day recorded, 'At 5.30 pm, as a result of enemy numerical superiority and flanking artillery fire from the north, the village had to be evacuated yet again. Weak elements hung on there, but the remainder had to pull back some 150 metres to the east. The falling of night precluded a further attempt at an assault. Order: The positions achieved are to be held in readiness for a continuation of the attack tomorrow.' All day on 2 November further attempts were taken to storm and hold Wytschaete. The British cavalry, which until then had fought hard to retain it, was finally and completely relieved by French troops. The main outcome of this change was that the

115

Wytschaete Hospice (in fact an agricultural school) in ruins. It had only been opened a few years at the outbreak of war.

French, having apparently decided that Wytschaete was not worth defending, pulled back and Bavarian Reserve Infantry Regiment 8 finally more or less walked in and took possession.

Due to the severe losses suffered by 6th Bavarian Reserve Division, it was decided that it was too risky to leave the division unreinforced, so 3rd Infantry Division was moved to the area and the Pomeranian Grenadier Regiments 2 and 9 force marched forward to take over the main responsibility from the largely fought-out Bavarians. Strangely the Bavarians were ambivalent about their arrival. For them it was a matter of honour for Bavarian troops to take and hold the village themselves and Grenadier Regiment 9 later stated that, 'On two separate occasions the order to 5 Infantry Brigade to attack was withdrawn, because the Bavarians wanted to storm Wytschaete alone'.

Bulfin's Force

It was hoped that the French would be able to launch a counter attack from both sides of the Comines Canal on **2 November**; Bulfin's troops were to conform. In fact, stymied by German artillery, they got nowhere, not even up to the line of the British trenches on the left. The German shelling caused most difficulties to the exposed position of 1/Irish Guards (1/IG); the shelling was followed up by an attack at about 11 am on Bulfin's force and the left of 7th Division. Bulfin sent in his only reserve, 26 Field Company, Lord Cavan despatched 2/Grenadiers and Haig sent half of his Corps Reserve, 6 (Cavalry) Brigade, to assist. At about noon Major General Bulfin was wounded and Lord Cavan assumed command: **(See map p. 118)**

I was walking with Frith and an orderly when a shell came and killed the orderly, smashed up Frith and I got hit in the head and

116

Ypres' Grand Place, already a ruin, in February 1915. The scaffolding on the Cloth Hall tower was already in place pre war.

side and so went down. I told Packenham to put the brigade under Lord Cavan and got away into Ypres after I had been patched up. Left Ypres that night, hospital being shelled, also the station. Our train badly shelled and several of the wounded killed.

The German attack continued to develop to the north, moving up towards 21 Brigade's positions; the right of the British line came under severe pressure at about 1 pm. The Irish Guards were forced to retire into the woods north of Klein Zillebeke and so the Ox & Bucks were forced to form a defensive right flank; but shortly afterwards the Northants were also forced back and so the battalion had to fall back to its reserve positions, where the line held. At the end of the day only this relatively small part of that morning's line had been lost, 7th Division having held fast.

During the day further French troops had either arrived or were close by, en route.

Lord Cavan's force had another hard morning. Heavy shelling forced the left company (adjacent to 20 Brigade) of the Northamptons out of their trenches at about 10.30 am and the battalion was withdrawn into the woods. He brought up his reserve and Major General Capper managed to scrape together more men to assist in holding the threatened part of the line – 2/Worcs, the Northumberland Hussars and the cyclist company. By 1 pm the Germans had worked forward and identified the apparent gap left by the Northamptons, only to be halted by the fire of the Northamptons and 2/Border of 20 Brigade. It was during this fighting that 20 Brigade lost its commander, Brigadier General Ruggles Brice, as the war diary records:

> *Chateau Heronthage* [sic]. *During a heavy shelling on our reserves ... was wounded in both arms and the shoulder blade.*

Further attacks at 4 pm and 6.15 pm petered out after only a matter of minutes; the British withdrew some of the reserves that had been sent forward and Capper felt secure enough to send back 7 (Cavalry) Brigade to his left, effectively restoring it to Haig's control.

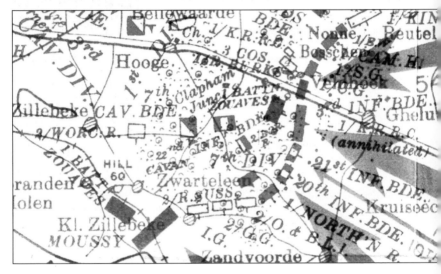

Situation of evening of 2 November between the canal and the Menin Road.

Chapter Three

The Last Days of the Battle

The next few days were quiet ones in this sector, although shelling continued. A certain amount of reorganisation took place and the 7th Division, in particular, received drafts, although at six officers and 694 men they hardly provided an adequate number given its losses. During this time, also, further French troops were earmarked for the sector, as Foch (who had been appointed Commandant du Groupe des Armées du Nord – GAN – on 11 October) reassured Haig on 4 November. On the other hand, on 5 November, Foch informed d'Urbal that major French offensive operations in Belgium were now over, as the Germans had established themselves too firmly.

It is important to remember that Messines Ridge was not the objective of the German attack at the end of October; it was merely intended to be an intermediate phase in the overall plan to achieve breakthrough south of Ypres. As a result Army Group Fabeck ordered a fresh all-out assault all along its front. Seeking to obtain one last maximum thrust from the men under his command, General der Infanterie von Deimling, commander XV Corps, issued a special Order of the Day that underlined that no stone was to be left unturned in the quest for vistory:

Ferdinand Foch.

Headquarters XV Corps Wervicq, 3 November 1914
Corps Order!

During the past three days the Corps has captured approximately forty officers and 2,000 British other ranks [Interesting to note the rather low number of claimed officer PoWs].

It is clear that the British surrender if they are subject to energetic attack.

I direct, therefore, that the attacks are to be pressed home with

General der Infanterie Berthold von Deimling, Commander XV Army Corps, during a visit to Field Artillery Regiment 80 in 1913.

bugle calls and with the regimental bands playing.
  Regimental musicians who play during assaults will be awarded Iron Crosses.
Signed: von Deimling

3 - 5 November: The Loss of Spanbroekmolen.

At Wytschaete, matters had become somewhat clearer, at least for the Germans. **3 November** had got off to a bad start for the German defenders. The French counter-attacked the northern part of the village, pushing Bavarian Reserve Infantry Regiment 8 back in places. This time, the regiment was quick to call for reinforcement by Grenadier Regiment 9 at about 2.00 pm to help throw back the attackers. Simultaneously, Grenadier Regiment 2 participated in a general attack thrust in the direction of Spanbroekmolen on the far side of the ridge between Messines and Wytschaete.

Unteroffizier Schadow, a member of 2nd Company Grenadier Regiment 2, subsequently provided a detailed description of this battle from his perspective.

Assault! What that word means to a soldier! To our front was a wide expanse of terrain. Wherever the eye could see shells and shrapnel rounds were exploding. First there would be a small cloud in the sky, then it would expand. Suddenly there would be

120

a roar and a rush of air, as though an autumn wind was blowing through the twigs. Over there a shell was landing in an isolated house. There was a dull but heavy crash and hundreds of tiles flew through the air. Where the house had once stood there was just a thick black cloud, enveloping red flames which shot skywards. So it was that something which a man had built by the sweat of his brow was flattened in an instant. The rafters still stuck up steeply, but they were being burnt higher and higher by the flames and it was not long until the whole place was one great inferno. Then there was a thunderous crash and only the blackened walls remained to bear witness that people had once lived here.

In the meantime we stayed in cover and thought once more about our own homes. Of course we knew that our thoughts could not dwell on that for long. Soon we should have to act and an iron sense of duty meant that we had to suppress all our humanity. The minutes ticked by with desperate slowness; time seemed to stretch out. We lay there completely still, looking so peaceful that it was hard to believe that all these men with their serious eyes would soon appear to be utterly transformed. Soon they would stretch their limbs and stand up, the light of battle in their eyes and their trusty weapons gripped tightly, ready to launch themselves wildly into battle. Above and around us raged the artillery battle. The earth seemed ready to burst as each side tried to out-do the other's firepower.

Everywhere where the shells landed they spread death and destruction, producing one glowing crater after another. The grim reaper moved amongst both friend and foe, young and old and claimed a rich harvest. The fire grew ever heavier, the sky was lit up as though by a sea of flames. It was as if the air was being split by hundreds of bolts of lightning – just a few moments now! – 'Fix bayonets!' That wrenched us out of our reverie. Already to our front the trumpets were sounding and the drums beating. Shouts of 'On your feet! Forwards!' rang in our ears. Off in front raced our first platoon, with Hauptmann von Waldow in the lead. With shells bursting in amongst them, they advanced in short bounds. It looked as though they had all disappeared off the face of the earth, as if they were all dead, but repeatedly the grey wave pushed on, pausing frequently to go to ground.

They finally set foot in the first abandoned line of trenches and were followed up by the Second Platoon and then the Third, though not all our comrades made it as far as the trench. But this was, in any case, no place to linger: press on was the watchword. We launched forward and all hell broke loose once more. Throwing ourselves down, we pressed our faces into the ground and gasped for breath. Then it was time for another bound. Shells crashed down on our ranks; here and there a comrade fell with Hurra! still on his lips. Forward, ever forward, we stormed at a breathless pace. Swift commands passed from mouth to mouth, but sometimes they could not be heard; the crash of the shells drowned everything else out. Rifle bullets whistled past us, punctuating the monotonous clatter of the machine guns. Out front our standard bearer (Hornack) went down passing, with the last of his strength, the unfurled colour to a comrade rushing forward to take it up.

Finally we could go no further and we leapt down into the enemy trenches. Tired out, we lay around or sat in an old position – played out men with restless eyes, staring around us, taking no note at all of shells or shrapnel – tired, just so tired! Evening fell. It went darker and darker then the moon rose and the artillery fire died away. Then stooped figures began moving over the bloody ground; the Samaritans of the battlefield. Here they would close the eyes of the dying, there they would offer a water bottle to a wounded man, who would take long draughts from it. 'Thank you, comrade!' We hunched down deeper into our coats and huddled together, but our tired bodies were shrieking for rest. We might have wanted to turn our thoughts to our homes once more but we were too tired, simply too tired. Now and again someone stirred, sighed deeply then slept on towards the morning that would bring further difficult tasks.

With the help of the Pomeranian troops, the situation in Wytschaete was swiftly rectified and, with a resumption of responsibility by Bavarian Reserve Infantry Regiment 8 for its forward defence, Grenadier Regiment 9 took advantage of the opportunity to allow its men to move into the cellars of the village and get some much needed rest overnight.

Fighting of varying degrees of intensity continued throughout the day along the Army Group Fabeck frontage, but there was barely any progress. The real problem was that the deployment in strength of French army units meant that the defence was stiffening by the day. However, attempts continued to be made for some time to come and on **4 November** 3rd Infantry Division tried again south of Wytschaete. Intense flanking fire meant that this attack faltered and then ground to a halt still about two hundred metres short of Hill 75 (ie Spanbroekmolen). Despite this check 3rd Battalion Grenadier Regiment 2, waiting in reserve, received orders just before midday to advance and it arrived forward by 2.00 pm. This renewed attack, which enjoyed fire support from the entire divisional artillery, further reinforced by the howitzer battery of Field Artillery Regiment 38, had an H Hour of 4.00 pm, but the almost inevitable complications meant that the start time had to be delayed until 5.00 pm.

Detailed accounts concerning this attack were written subsequently by some of the survivors. These included Leutnant von Kleist of 8th Company:

We officers wished each other luck, drank a last schnaps and smoked a final cigarette then, punctually at 5.00 pm, the trumpeters blew, 'Fix bayonets!' and a crazy rate of fire was opened. However, because visibility was so poor, nobody could really tell what they were firing at. Five minutes later the order to attack was given and the wild hunt was on. The first objective was a farmstead. What did we care about the artillery? What did it matter who was firing at the farmstead: ours, or the enemy's? The [enemy] had certainly spotted our advance, countering it with a hail of lead and iron. It was complete hell, but we pressed forward and had soon taken the first farmstead. However, shells were coming down accurately and men fell as though they had been mown down. I indicated the second target with my sword, but my arm fell as though it had been paralysed. I put away my sword and pistol and carried on. There was a hedge twenty metres to my front – but what was that? I stumbled on and threw myself down by the hedge. My foot had also been hit and I stayed lying where I was.

Kriegsfreiwilliger von Geibler, also of 8th Company recalled:

It was midday. We were still under cover in the trench. Finally – about 4.00 pm – a runner arrived from Leutnant von Kleist. 'The platoon is to prepare to advance. Move forward to the trench which is currently under fire, then go half right towards a farm – a watermill – and assemble there! The other platoons will be following up!' At long last the relief of an end to all the waiting, to having to lie still. Now it was up and at the enemy! I can still see them in my mind's eye, all my mates, moving on past the 3rd Battalion and shouting wisecracks and jokes at them, like

123

acquaintances from an exercise as they lay at readiness lining the edge of a sunken road. The move continued. At one point contact was lost between two sections, but this was restored and first the platoon, then the whole company, arrived at the farm. Leutnant von Kleist lay together with Hauptmann von Mutius in a large hole in the ground which had once been a clamp for sugar beet.

I ran over to him and reported all present. He gave out his orders then I heard Hauptmann von Mutius shout over to the trumpeter: 'Blow, Fix bayonets! and put the wind up that lot over there!' At that the trumpeters took up the call which ran along from the right, echoing back quietly amongst the noise of the firing. There was great enthusiasm, almost jubilation, amongst us as bayonets flew out of their scabbards, then it was, 'On your feet, forwards!' and we advanced on the enemy. Initially my platoon advanced half right through a hollow, then straight on and through a hedge – but where was the enemy? They had pulled back. Nevertheless we [received] fire from the front and the flanks and salvoes of shells fell around and amongst us. We lay there for a short while and then dashed further on.

To our right was a platoon from another company. I was just about to order another bound forward when shrapnel burst overhead, throwing me to one side. I felt dizzy and faint, but pulled myself together and shouted at the man next to me that I was wounded and that the next most senior Unteroffizier was to assume command. It was not until late in to the night that the wounded were all brought in to the dressing station at Bas-Warneton and there I met up with some comrades from the company. All the platoon commanders of 8th Company had been hit, as had the company commander, Leutnant von Kleist, who took his sword in his left hand after he had been hit and continued to charge forwards until he was wounded again.

Here, as in so many other places along the Western Front, the law of diminishing returns had begun to apply. Huge efforts were being made **See map p. 147** for small gains at great cost. Nevertheless, the pattern of attacks continued for several more days. Grenadier Regiment 9 also became involved, as did Infantry Regiment 42, the other regiment of 3rd Division, after **6 November**.

As late as 5 November, in fact, d'Urbal had some hopes of removing the Germans from Messines Ridge. For example, on that day his staff was busy arranging a new attack on Messines. Scheduled to begin at 7 am, in fact it was delayed until 3 pm. The Germans, however, launched their own attack before then and by 5 pm had pushed the French off Spanbroekmolen and a kilometre beyond.

The new line to the west of Messines Ridge that was now more or less 'finally' established meant that the Cavalry Corps connected to it at almost a right angle.

Elsewhere, to the north, on **5 November** heavy shelling caused Lord Cavan's battalions to take shelter in the woods behind. The best that could be said about the last few days was that the weather had been kind, often with clear, sunny weather – although of course this meant that the nights were cold. The 7th Division, at long last, was relieved, a process that took until the early hours of 6 November, by ten battalions of II Corps – II Corps itself having been partially relieved five days earlier from its line north of Givenchy by the Indian Corps.

French met his Corps commanders at Bailleul (just over the border, to the west of Kemmel) on the 5th; there was a feeling that the worst was over and much of the discussion was about leave arrangements and wintering in the field. The GHQ British intelligence summary for that day, however, suggested that all might well not be over.

Meanwhile, d'Urbal issued instructions for the 6th to his command to continue limited offensives, north and south of Klein Zillebeke, seeking to expand the narrow salient around the village.

Situation evening/early morning 5/6 November. Note the strength of French troops south west of St Eloi.

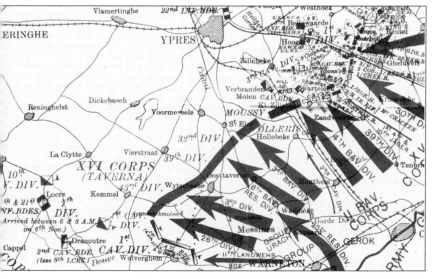

6 – 11 November: The struggle north of the Comines Canal

This was a bad day for the Anglo-French forces around Klein Zillebeke. The French, under the command of Moussy, along with Lord Cavan's force on the left, lost considerable ground. The Germans attacked in the fog, anticipating a French offensive and supported by an artillery bombardment that had been both persistent and effective. The woods west of Hollebeke as well as the canal tunnel were lost, whilst two chasseur battalions 'were seized with inexplicable panic and abandoned nearly a mile of ground' east of St Eloi. A firm grip had to be taken of them before they returned to attempt to recapture it. Eikhof Farm was lost.

North of the canal the French 90th Regiment suffered very badly in the bombardment, losing two companies to it at about 10 am. At 2.30 pm, the ground being held until then by the Irish Guards and 2/Grenadiers, a heavy infantry attack was launched against the French on the right, making use of saps driven during the night from their trenches. The line was broken in three places and the French started to drift back towards Zillebeke. The Irish Guards were forced back on their flank at first and then the rest of the position collapsed, with a withdrawal that went beyond the support line. 2/Grenadiers held on, but suffered substantial casualties during the day. Reinforcements from 2/Sussex and the Ox & Bucks stabilised the right flank, however, but without being able to seal the gap to the south. The German advance continued, reaching Zwarteleen and almost to Verbrandenmolen. Once aware of the gravity of the situation, Lord Cavan ordered 7 (Cavalry) Brigade to halt the Germans. Brigadier General Kavanagh took his brigade, mounted, to the south east, across the French line of retreat. A squadron of the Royal Horse Guards (RHGs, often known as the Blues) were despatched to cover his right and he dismounted 1 and 2/Life Guards and the remainder of the RHGs and advanced on Zwarteleen. Meanwhile General Moussy, with the few reserves he had available, in a manoeuvre of which the personally reckless Marshal Ney would have been proud, led them forward with his sword in hand on the right of 7 Brigade. Zwarteleen and the woods to the left were cleared and the cavalry reached the Irish Guards' old line; whilst the French went on to attempt the recovery of their former line. They were driven off, taking with them some of the British cavalry on their left. The situation was finally stabilised on the western outskirts of the hamlet of Zwarteleen, but at a considerable cost, including Lieutenant Colonel Wilson of the RHGs and Major Dawnay, commanding 2/Life Guards, killed; as well as Lieutenant Wyndham, mentioned earlier. (Wyndham and Wilson were buried in Zillebeke Churchyard, but Dawney is to be found in Harlebeke New British Cemetery, many miles away. This cemetery includes concentrations from German cemeteries, particularly of British October 1914 casualties; likely he died of wounds in a German hospital or clearing station, or was removed for burial some distance to the rear.) The cavalry had particularly heavy losses amongst officers, with seventeen casualties, along with seventy eight other ranks; nevertheless, the action provides a fine example of the ability of the cavalry to act as a 'fire brigade', dealing with dangerous situations by an ability to move quickly and then to act effectively in an infantry role.

At 3.25 pm Haig sent what were, in terms of the overall situation, substantial reinforcements – about a thousand men in the end, the total strength of the four battalions concerned at that time. The intention was to counter attack and restore the situation, at least at Zwarteleen, but an attack could only be launched at 6 pm and the move by 2/Glosters and 2/KRRC failed. Lord Cavan decided that nothing useful would be gained by further fighting in the dark and so the line was reorganised. 3 Brigade now held the position from the railway bridge near Hill 60, through the western edge of Zwarteleen and on to Lord Cavan's right flank. Haig's final reinforcements were most welcome. 2/Munsters had been destroyed in what is called 'The Affair at Etreux', on 27 August, during the Retreat. It had been completely rebuilt subsequently and had been engaged in preparing rear lines. This 800 strong battalion now went into the line, at about 6.30 pm, between 3 Brigade and Lord Cavan's troops. Meanwhile, the poor old 22 Brigade, hardly relieved from the days of hard fighting it had undergone, was brought up to Zillebeke, arriving at about 10 pm. Thus the Germans had made a very convincing push on 6 November, driving a wedge between the British and French forces and having almost taken St Eloi and brought their line forward to within a few thousand metres of Ypres by the canal.

7 November started misty: as the *OH* says, 'it marked the definite commencement of the winter weather: mud henceforth seriously interfered with operations, and the cold at night made sleeping in the open difficult, if not impossible'. Haig was severely concerned by the situation around the canal, fearing that he would have to withdraw his whole line back so that it ran through Ypres. The French reassured him in the early hours of the morning and Moussy was able, albeit with very weak forces, to re-establish contact with French troops on his right, taking up a line parallel to the road leading to the tunnel under the canal. That he was able to do so was largely a consequence of the complete lack of Germans on the ground when he made the move, presumably preoccupied with the fighting further north. French intentions were to reoccupy their old line north of the canal – indeed Foch thought that this had been done by 9.30

am – but there were insufficient reinforcements to attempt this until 5.30 pm and by then it was both too dark and Cavan's troops in the line were too exhausted from fighting earlier in the day to be able to participate.

Lord Cavan had decided that he had to take action early on 7 November. The counter attack that he had in mind would be led by Brigadier General Lawford's 22 Brigade, which by this stage was reduced to only fourteen officers. At 4 am he sent the brigade forward, via a path in the woods, to the junction of his force with 3 Brigade, placing it forward of 3 Brigade's left flank, where it made use of a rise in the ground for cover. The attack was launched at 6.15 am against the German line, which lay 150 yards away, partly in the open and partly in woods. 2/Queen's were on the left, 1/S Staffs on the right and 2/Warwicks in reserve; unfortunately the firing of a gun to signal the start of the advance and for all troops to take part in it was not at all satisfactory – the sound could not be distinguished from the rest of the racket going on at the time. The result was that only 1/Glosters actually joined in from 3/Brigade. The consequence was that only the first line of German defences were occupied; by 4 pm – dusk - there was no sign of the French coming up on the right and there was a danger of the position being overwhelmed by Germans coming around the open flanks, particularly on the right. Thus the men were brought back to the original line, and from there to the reserve, having lost 304 other ranks and ten officers, leaving the brigade with only four. Amongst those killed was Captain JF Vallentin of 1/S Staffs, who was awarded the VC in February 1915; he is commemorated on the Menin Gate. His citation reads:

For conspicuous bravery on 7th November, at Zillebeke. When leading the attack against the Germans under a very heavy fire he was struck down, and on rising to continue the attack was immediately killed. The capture of the enemy's trenches which followed was in a great measure due to the confidence which the men had in their Captain, arising from his many previous acts of great bravery and ability.

In 4th Division's sector, the German attack there resulted in the capture of the eastern part of the hamlet of Le Gheer.

On the morning of **8 November**, Haig and French met Foch at his headquarters at Cassel. It

Captain John Vallentin.
© Taylor Library

was an unsatisfactory meeting, because Foch could not promise any immediate French reinforcements. In addition Haig was concerned, a concern shared by Sir John French, by the dangerous situation near the Comines Canal:

> *... where General Moussy had not recovered the lost ground, so that the enemy was within two miles of Ypres; they emphasised that the safety of the British forces to the northward and the communications of all the troops under Sir D Haig, which passed through Ypres, depended on a weak French detachment, over which GOC I Corps had no control. A short advance there would result in all his command being cut off.*

Foch said that he had ordered the line to be restored but was not informed what the actual position of the French line might be. French repeated to Haig that he could deal directly with General d'Urbal, commanding the French Eighth Army. The end result as regards 8 November was that the French line advanced up to the canal line but no advance was made on the left, so that Cavan's right flank was still at an awkward right angle. To the rear, a couple of French territorial battalions dug trenches along the line Voormezeele - Zillebeke - Hooge. The French 11th Division was also moved, to the right rear of St Eloi. French probes along the line got nowhere. Along the south of the British line there was little change; 4th Division failed to eject the Germans from Le Gheer whilst, despite considerable and justifiable anxiety, no attempt was made against the perilous position of Lord Cavan's force. The relative calm did lead to a turnover of his troops: Cavan felt that practically all his men in the line were in need of a minimum of twenty four hours of respite.

Despite all attempts by the German army to press on with their advance in the Bavarian II Corps area, as the first week in November drew to a close there were no more gains of significance and the opposing front lines began to assume the shape they were to retain for many months to come. The situation was much the same in the XV Corps area, where progress along the line of the Menin Road became glacial in its slowness. Nevertheless, with everything being risked on forcing a decision around Ypres, the various formations continued to be called on for 'one final effort'.

See map p. 138

One of the very last operations associated specifically with Army Group Fabeck took place on **8 November**. Infantry Regiment 136, commanded by Major von Trott, was nearing complete exhaustion after days of heavy fighting and the associated casualties, (no fewer than eleven officers, thirteen *Offizierstellvertreter*s and 829 other ranks, or approximately one third of its entire strength). As an emergency measure, the survivors were formed into two composite battalions and its numbers were boosted by the arrival of reinforcements, most of whom were *Kriegsfreiwilligers* [wartime volunteers], who had left their studies at the University of Göttingen. Offizierstellvertreter Böttcher Infantry Regiment 136, who was closely involved with this new development, wrote a detailed account of his experience of this chaotic and inconclusive action and the days that led up to it.

We set out during the evening of Monday 2 November 1914. Six companies of Kriegsfreiwilligers and Ersatz Reservists, some of whom had travelled with me from Infantry Regiment 82 in Göttingen, had been brought together at Strasbourg. Commanded by Hauptmann Nelle, who had already been awarded the Iron Cross First and Second Class, they had carried out tactical exercises and some shooting. Now, after about twelve weeks of training, they were to be sent to reinforce XV Corps, which had suffered severe losses. Having detrained in Lille and spent the night in a school near the memorial to Joan of Arc, they marched via Wervicq, where there was another overnight halt, as far as Amerika [two and a half kilometres north of Wervicq]. *Here the reinforcements were finally allocated to companies. During the evening of 5 November orders arrived to move forward to the positions of Infantry Regiment 136; that is to say to the trenches.*

Under the cover of darkness we set off, guided by an Unteroffizier who knew the area and who had been sent back by the regiment. All we knew was that it was in the direction of Ypres. The main road to Ypres was teeming with arms and services of every kind, as well as field kitchens, ammunition columns etc. Every now and then a shell impacted somewhere nearby. Had the enemy fired more, the situation on that broad road would have been terrible, packed as it was in the darkness. We marched almost as far as Gheluvelt and then turned off to the left along a track where the mud was almost up to our calves and we had to be careful that we did not stumble into a shell hole and drown. Picking our way carefully through the darkness we passed fields, ditches, meadows and other obstacles, until we reached a small copse, where we paused.

An Offizierstellvertreter of the troops already in position was ordered to spread the newly arrived reinforcements around some of the trenches of the second line. In the darkness of the wood that was no easy task and each of us was happy if we managed to avoid deep holes. I was put in charge of one detachment and was told to deploy them in a particular trench that was already partly full of water. However, bullets whistling past now and then ensured that the men had soon disappeared into the depths. My young soldier-students wanted to know, naturally, where and how far away the enemy were, what the situation was and what role was intended for us. All I knew was that we were in the second line. Our guns were located a short distance behind us. Every time they fired the ground trembled and in response a 'blessing' was sent howling towards us from over there. It was certainly a thorough grounding in warlike operations for us.

About midday on 6 November we were assembled on a narrow path in the wood then, together with experienced men, were sent to the various rifle companies. Our company, the 4th, was directed to a position on a wooded forward slope. To our front a clearing opened up. The British were supposed to be located on the far side of it. The troops to our left were more or less level with us but, to our right, the battalion was rather more to the rear. A British attack was expected that evening and soon the first shots rang out. Platoon Commander Kulawik was first to spot the danger and shouted, 'Half right, 300 – 400 metres, British troops in the scrub by the clearing! Rapid fire!' Someone shouted back to Leutnant Schott, 'We are under heavy enfilade fire!' We barely had time to take cover in the positions we had prepared and to bring our rifles into our shoulders. After we had been pinned down in this murderous flanking fire for several minutes, a call came, 'About turn, take cover in the thicker wood to the rear!'

At that everyone flooded to the rear, bent over and pushing through the scrub for about two hundred metres, in order to be able to man a front facing the enemy, who were attacking from the right. We thought it terrible that our first experience of battle was to turn our backs on the enemy. However, the weight of British fire increased. An absolute hail of fire whistled over our heads, striking left and right of us. To add to our enjoyment we came under heavy shrapnel fire as well. Suddenly, however, both the shrapnel and small arms fire died away. Some way off I heard Hauptmann Nelle order an assault. Immediately there were repeated shouts of Hurra! and heavy small arms fire broke out, the sound gradually dying away as it became more distant. Night fighting in woods is always a grisly business, especially when it begins with an enemy ambush. The British had to evacuate the high wood, but our casualties were also heavy. Hauptmann Nelle, leading from the front, was wounded in the shoulder right at the start and a great many of the volunteers were killed.

We occupied the holes and trenches that the British had evacuated but, unfortunately, we could do nothing for the wounded, because a renewed attack was expected at any moment. Here we passed four days and four nights, at times experiencing Hell on earth. The shell and shrapnel fire which lashed us and felled the trees around us was dreadful. It was particularly bad that there were no medical orderlies with us and first aid had to be administered by platoon and section commanders, whilst the evacuation of the severely wounded had to be carried out by the infantrymen themselves. This could only be done at night, because anybody showing himself by day was immediately fired on. This was the time when Unteroffizier Heß, who carried out the duties of company feldwebel here forward, was killed whilst observing. He was the only regular unteroffizier in the entire company. Offizierstellvertreter Kulawik was so severely wounded in the head that he died whilst he was being evacuated. My faithful batman, Schweineberg, was also slightly wounded.

Our artillery managed to land several direct hits in the British trenches, forcing them to pull back into the reserve trenches in rear. Naturally we exploited this opportunity to fire on those retreating. Schweineberg, joining in, was just about to fire when, a British soldier swung round in a standing position suddenly and shot at him. He immediately felt a burning sensation in his head, but luckily the bullet had only creased him. This accuracy shown by the long service British soldiers with colonial experience, who were deployed opposite the company, verged on the miraculous. On the morning of the fourth day we heard that we were to be relieved that evening at 8.00 pm. However, the closer we drew to that hour, the more critical the situation became. Intense artillery fire began to come down on and around us and crash followed crash, as shells impacted very close by, causing the earth to tremble and walls to crumble. Splinters and bullets flew in all directions and the machine gun, which was laid along the line of the communication trench, began to play its music with fresh intensity. Minute after minute dragged by, each seeming like an eternity. But we were in luck. The thunder of the enemy artillery did not last long. Betrayed by their muzzle flashes, our guns began to fire back accurately and so increasingly gagged the enemy. Finally our relief took place at about midnight.

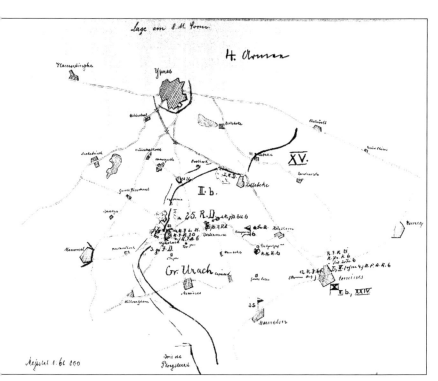

Army Group Fabeck overall situation on 8 November 1914.

In the course of **8 November** the French took over 2/KRRC's position on the extreme right, near Hill 60; 3 Brigade – all of 500 strong – was relieved by 500 men of 3rd (Cavalry) Division; the London Scottish replaced 2/Sussex and 2/Ox & Bucks; the 800 men of 22 Brigade were withdrawn at night to Locre, leaving the Irish Guards, reorganised into two weak companies, and 2/Grenadiers in the line. Haig also tried to reorganise his divisions so that the composite parts, which had become scattered, could be brought back together to their original formations, but this could only partially be effected. Meanwhile, intelligence continued to show that the Germans appeared to be continuing to concentrate troops near Ypres. Despite the overall unpromising situation, at Supreme Army Headquarters and as described in the companion guide *Menin Road 1914*, efforts were still being made as late as 10 November to introduce fresh troops in the hope of forcing a decision but, at Headquarters Army Group Fabeck, both the commander and chief of staff had been quite certain a full week previously that the situation was hopeless and that there was no prospect in the current circumstances of achieving any sort of breakthrough. On 8 November, elements of XV Corps did capture

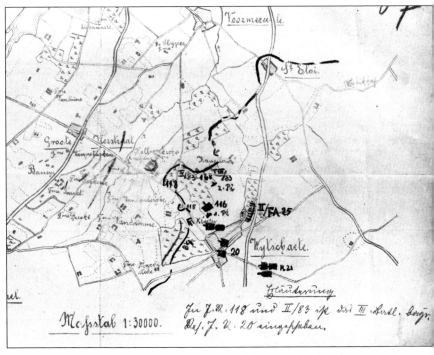

The front line northwest of Wytschaete, following the abortive attack by 25th Reserve Division on 8 November.

Veldhoek, but the advance of II Bavarian Army Corps, in the *Schwerpunkt* of Army Group Fabeck, had not only stalled, it was also under great pressure from British counter-attacks directed at 6th Bavarian Reserve Division. There was some local fighting for tactical advantage, but the guns had hardly any shells left, so the entire load fell on the infantry, which suffered high casualties as a result.

However, **9th November** was also quiet. A contributing factor to this lull might have been that the weather for the last couple of days had precluded aerial observation; this did not seem to effect the continuous shelling by the Germans. The French troops under General Grossetti [of XVI Corps], positioned between British I and III Corps, were reorganised into a number of groups as, like the British, their usual divisional and brigade organisation had been disrupted by the need to send men piecemeal to parts of the line as required. They still had time to regain some ground near St Eloi and Spanbroekmoelen. The Irish Guards were at long last relieved, by 1/SWB. Perhaps most importantly, it was agreed between d'Urbal and Haig that the British reserve would be held on the Menin Road and the French on the Zillebeke Road.

Although **10 November** was quiet for the British, this was far from being the case for the French on the left, who were fiercely attacked from Langemarck to Dixmuide. There was a considerable bombardment during the night and the infantry assault, by *Fourth Army*, that followed at about 1 pm resulted in the capture of the Dixmuide bridgehead (although the Germans could not retain a toehold on the west side of the Yser), ground north west of Bixschoote, Kortekeer Cabaret, some trenches west of Langemarck and pushed French troops either up to or across the Yser Canal. Thus d'Urbal had to despatch whatever reserves that he could spare from those held near Zillebeke. The effect was that the French, perhaps justifiably, felt that the decisive blow was to fall on the left flank. This potentially disastrous conclusion meant that there was now minimal support for the relatively weak French front at and to the west of the Comines Canal. Perhaps fortune smiled on the allies; it appears that the original intention of the Germans was to launch a major attack all along the front but with the principal effort being astride the Menin Road. However, because weather had delayed reconnaissance and other arrangements, matters were not sufficiently in hand to satisfy von Plettenberg, commander of the Guards Corps, for an assault astride the Menin Road on the 10th. One wonders what might have happened if the whole attack had indeed been carried out simultaneously instead of across two days.

11 November

At first light on a grey, foggy morning, at 6.30 am, the German artillery opened up – 'the most terrific fire that the British had experienced', growing in intensity before 9 am, the time when the infantry assault was to begin. The shelling and that of previous days was to prove something of a mixed blessing, as it had so torn up the woods as to make the resultant chaos of branches, stumps and shell holes a most effective obstacle when marked by rifle fire. The soldiers at the receiving end could do little else except get as low into the ground as possible and wait.

In front of Messines the Germans, although supposed to attack, did not do so, apparently as a consequence of the weight of the allied artillery on their positions. Between Allenby's left and the Comines Canal there was a lot of firing of small arms but no change in the line. North of the canal, however, the French came under considerable pressure, especially as a significant part of their reserves had been shifted to the north the previous day. At about noon the line began to give way. There was no help available – the situation on the Menin Road had swallowed up almost all of the reserves. It was General Dubois who

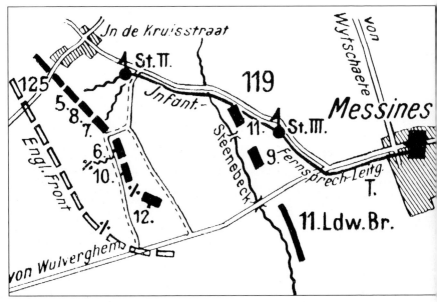

Company defensive positions Grenadier Regiment 119, mid November 1914, west of Messines.

was able to come to the rescue, sending a cavalry regiment from St Jean. Leaving their horses at Zillebeke, they made a counter attack which succeeded in establishing a line from Spoil Bank Railway Bridge-Verbrandenmolen-Zwarteleen by 6.30 pm. However this was not the end of the fighting in the Zwarteleen - Hill 60 sector. The following day, **12 November**, a serious attempt by assorted formations and units of the German 30th and 39th Infantry Divisions saw the start of an intense period of fighting, which culminated in the capture and temporary securing of Hill 60 by the time that Commander *Fourth Army* called off offensive operations on 17 November.

Lord Cavan's force suffered chiefly from artillery fire during **11 November**, along with rifle fire that was, however, generally aimed too high. The biggest problem faced the London Scottish, split in two with 2/Munsters and 2/Welch in between. First the right flank was threatened with envelopment, but the situation there would be saved by a counter attack by men from the neighbouring battalion, 2/KRRC; then the left part of the battalion faced similar problems, but this was resolved by Lieutenant Colonel Malcolm bringing up the men of his headquarters into the line.

Further north, between Shrewsbury Forest and the right flank of 3rd Division (Major General F Wing, killed in action in October 1915), the

136

Command post Infantry Regiment 126 39th Infantry Division near Klein Zillebeke in November. Left to right, Oberleutnant Vischer, Major Goez and Reserve Leutnant Haidlen.

German assault also had little impact. Wing's division had been split into three groups, from north to south: Brigadier General McCracken's, comprising 2/KOSB – fresh from Neuve Chapelle, 2/R Irish Rifles, and 1/Gordons, with 1/S Lancs and 1/Wilts in reserve; Brigadier General Count Gleichen's, with 1/Cheshire and 2/Beds; and Brigadier General Shaw's, comprising 1/Lincolns, I/N Fus, 4/R Fusiliers and a Zouave company, with 1/RSF in reserve up to the Menin Road, whilst north of the road were 2/Duke of Wellington's. The *OH* describes the attack on the two groups nearest Cavan's men, beginning by quoting from the German semi official account, published during the war, *Ypres 1914*:

> ... *'great difficulties were encountered. Deep trenches, broad obstacles [formed entirely by their own artillery fire] and enfilade*

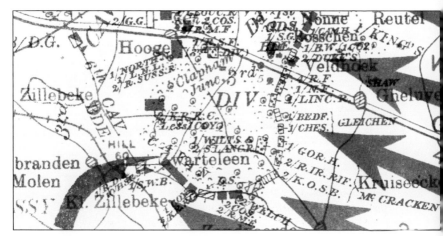

Situation east of Hill 60 morning of 11 November.

machine gun fire combined to make progress slow, especially on the right wing.' There was, in fact, no progress whatever. Advancing slowly, after the first staggering blow of a minute's British rapid fire, in what appeared to be many lines, with their rifles at the secure under their arms, 'without enthusiasm and in a sort of dazed way as if they were drugged' – as it was reported by one British battalion – the Prussians [of 4th Division], scourged by the shrapnel of the 1st Divisional artillery, broken and rebroken by rifle fire, fell back to shelter again.

Further advances were broken up, mainly by artillery fire; the last attack was at 4 pm, 'but not a German approached the British trenches'. By 9 pm all was quiet on the front of McCracken's and Gleichen's groups. It was a different story for Shaw's group, whose battalions straddled the Menin Road.

Shaw's Group
The attack here, as elsewhere, commenced at about 9 am. The earlier German shelling seems to have been heaviest against this group and McCracken's to the south. The shelling had already turned 4/R Fusiliers out of their front line positions near the Menin Road, but they were still able to fend off the Germans' initial attack. However, German success in getting into the British line north of the road (see *The Menin Road* in this series), meant that the battalion was under attack in enfilade and from the front and the men fell back, along with the Zouaves to the north. In the process of trying to restore the situation, Brigadier General N McMahon was killed: appointed to the command of 10 Brigade, he was still with

4/R Fusiliers, his old battalion. Captain O'Donel, the adjutant of the battalion, says of the day:

> *Still in the same position. Terrible shelling started about 6.30 am and continued for about two and a half hours (this is much the worst shelling I have seen during the war). Infantry attack followed (it is said by the 15th Battalion of the German Imperial Guard –* in fact probably 4th (Queen Augusta's) Guard Grenadiers*) and our line was driven in to a certain extent, but by the help of a very determined counter attack by the Royal Scots Fusiliers and supported by the Royal Sussex Regiment the line was held. Colonel McMahon (now Brigadier General) was killed.*

The Royal Fusiliers' regimental history notes that he was on the east side of Herenthage Wood:

> *The front trenches were knocked to pieces, and many of the men were killed or wounded. Captain Routley, in command, tried to send back a report on the plight of his men, but it was impossible to live in such a bombardment. Then followed the infantry attack ... the little band of men received the first assault with the bayonet and hurled it back. Routley, about this time, was the only officer left and he was wounded in the head. The Grenadiers delivered a second charge. Some of the men were driven from their trenches, and their appearance in the rear created a panic among the battalion supports, who appear to have been chiefly special reservists, a draft who arrived on the day before the battle and had not yet been organised into their platoons. Colonel [sic] McMahon went to them and tried to rally them. Suddenly he was seen to sink on one knee and began to remove his legging as though hit in the leg. At that moment a shell burst close to him and killed him.*

For reasons that are obscure, McMahon, who has no known grave, is commemorated on the Memorial to the Missing near Ploegsteert, rather than on the Menin Gate.

Shaw sent up 1/RSF and 2/Sussex; two companies of the former caught the Germans in the flank as they had turned southwards into the wood, presumably in an attempt to roll up the British line from the north. This they succeeded in doing, though they were able to observe the strange sensation that whilst they were pushing the Germans eastwards, they could see other Germans advancing westwards on the other side of the Menin Road. At first it was reported that the RSF had recaptured 4/R Fusiliers' original position, but in fact they had retaken the support line, two hundred yards behind. This was the sole German gain on the day on this part of the front.

In the midst of all of this, at about 10 am, Shaw himself was wounded when in an estaminet just east of Hooge:

> Brigadier General Shaw, his staff captain, Lieutenant Harter and the Signalling Officer, Lieutenant Deakin, were wounded by a shell about 10 am.

Command went to Lieutenant Colonel W Smith of the Royal Sussex. Shaw, then 53 years old, recovered and went on to command 13th (Western) Division at Gallipoli.

The Fusiliers' regimental history provides a commentary on subsequent events. That evening there were only two officers and fifty men that could be gathered; by the following evening there were a hundred and by the 13th, still with only two officers, 170 men. The battalion had a nervy time in the trenches before Kemmel at the end of the month and went through some difficult times, doubtless an experience shared by many battalions as they attempted to rebuild after the shattering early months of the war.

> But on the 27th [November] the battalion had to take over the trenches at Kemmel from the Norfolks. It was the last test to apply to men so little accustomed to warfare; but the days were critical and such risks had to be taken. Major Hely Hutchinson [the new CO] had to deal with some serious cases of nerves, but under his firm hand the unit settled down, and spent three days in the trenches. ... The trenches had been wet, and many of the men had bad feet. Moreover, the shortage of NCOs made discipline a little slack. One can hardly wonder at this. The battalion had been wiped out twice since the opening of the war. In these four months they had lost 1,900 NCOs and men and over fifty officers, killed, wounded, sick and missing. These figures must surely be unique!

The German communiqué for 11 November possibly says it all by not saying much:

> In the neighbourhood east of Ypres our troops advanced further. A total of more than seven hundred Frenchmen were taken, as well as four guns and four machine guns.

The British do not rate a mention, either on the 11th or on the 12th.

12th November to the departure of the BEF from the Ypres Salient.
Although we now know that 11 November was the last date on which the British line was seriously threatened, this is with the advantage of hindsight. The condition of the BEF was dire – as for all combatants, of course, in the sector.

> *The weather by this time had turned thoroughly wintry. Cold and rain on the 12th, 13th and 14th were followed ... by a little snow on the 15th. Then came frost at night, hard frost on the 18th, six hours of snow storm on the 19th and snow covering the ground on the 20th. Apart from the discomfort of the troops thus occasioned, and the first appearance of frost bite from their standing in trenches half full of water, the physical condition of the men was becoming desperate. The strain of fighting so many days in succession was at last beginning to tell seriously. Men were reported to be standing up in their trenches fast asleep under fire, although the opposing infantry was only a hundred or so yards away, and grenade throwing and sniping made it nearly impossible to obtain regular rest. The ground was now a sea of mud and, although as mentioned, some of the roads had been corduroyed* [ie laid out with halved tree trunks, creating a ribbed effect – much hard work done on this under the direction of Brigadier General Rice, Chief Engineer I Corps, who had also organised a highly effective traffic management scheme], *the paths through the woods leading up to the front and the tracks by the side of the roads were so soft that men literally sank to their knees in them.*

On a positive note, 8th Division, almost entirely composed of returning regular units from colonial stations, completed its concentration in France on 13 November.

Meanwhile the fight to control Hill 60 continued in the days following 11 November. Despite being worn down by the recent struggles and having suffered severe losses, several units in succession were thrown into the battle. Eventually the original exhausted troops of XV Corps were relieved in the line by men of 19th Infantry Division, which had been subordinated to it for the purpose. Prior to the deployment of the latter formation, however, it had already taken almost all the ground of tactical importance on and around the hill. Infantry Regiment 132 of 39th Division played a prominent role in these

141

operations, but to 3rd Battalion Infantry Regiment 143 of 30th Infantry Division belongs the lion's share of the credit for the capture of Hill 60 itself, between 12 and 15 November. Reserve Leutnant Hagedorn, commanding 10th Company Infantry Regiment 143, later described events from his perspective:

The assault of the 132nd [on **13 November**] *went in straight across open ground, but was unable to reach its objective. About seventy five metres short of Hill 60 the attackers were halted by British fire and forced to dig in. However, the importance of the hill demanded that the attack be continued ... 10th Company, which was still lining the edge of the wood, was ordered to advance by sections and occupy a trench about eighty metres behind the front line. From there the entire company was to advance in bounds, take cover in front of the troops located there and incorporate them in the assault, which was to be supported by 11th Company ... The plan was good, but failed due to the strength and watchfulness of the British.*

10th Company set off at 1.00 pm, reaching the first trench with no problem ... but then the assault was launched over ground which lay open like an unfolded map before the eyes of the alert British troops. I commanded the first rush and leapt out of the trench at the head of the company. Immediately the British infantry brought down fire heavy enough to cause painful casualties. 'Take cover!' I shouted then, after a short breather, 'On your feet! Double march!' Once more the company rose as one man and rushed forward. From the right hand side of the road could be heard the voice of Oberleutnant Borck, but his voice was gradually drowned in the swelling enemy fire which constantly tore new holes in the lines and forced the company to take cover in the forward trench. But the well aimed shots of the enemy proved more powerful than the words of command, making it impossible to leave the trench ... The company was tangled up with disorganised elements of Infantry Regiment 132 and it was impossible to get any further forward in daylight.

It was agreed to continue the attack as it was going dark ... as night began to fall the attack was relaunched. This was not an attack with shouts of 'Hurra!', rifles at the ready; rather it was a matter of creeping forward silently to the edge of the crest ... there was a steep sided two metre bank, the troops pushed on a few metres and dug in, in the belief that the much sought after hill was theirs. It was impossible to see in the darkness that the actual summit, which offered the desirable long views, was actually twenty metres further on. The mistake was not noticed until the following morning [14 November]. It was a serious disappointment for 3rd Battalion, even though this partial success was fully acknowledged by the higher commanders.

Gradually, over the next couple of days, Infantry Regiment 77, which relieved Infantry Regiment 143 during the night **14/15 November**, consolidated the somewhat tenuous German hold on Hill 60. Possession of the crest was disputed with the French army until 10 December, after which German units retained it until the battles of mid-April 1915.

(See map p. 194)

So far as the allies were concerned, these post 11 November days brought the odd alarm, occasionally quite a serious one, south of the Menin Road. On **12 November** Moussy's men were shelled out of Zwarteleen, which impacted on Cavan's right flank. Some men from

Situation 30th Infantry Division Klein Zillebeke 19 November.

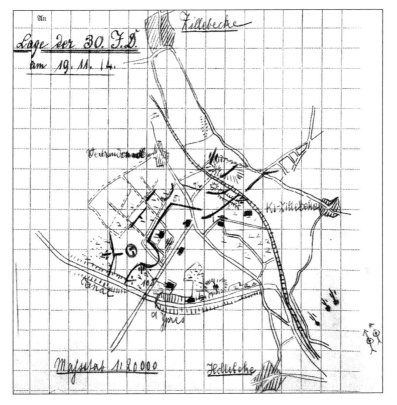

143

2/KRRC were sent to cover the gap, in the course of which Second Lieutenant Dimmer won the VC. He had charge of four machine guns; German shelling killed three of his men and he himself was severely wounded; he managed, however, to man a gun himself and inflicted severe damage on the Germans. His VC was gazetted on 19 November, ie a week after the action – although he did not know about it until he saw a report in a newspaper a week after that. He wrote to his mother about the fighting:

> *I got my guns going, but they smashed up one almost immediately, and then turned all their attention on the gun I was with, and succeeded in smashing that too, but before they completed the job I had been twice grounded and was finally knocked out with the gun. My face is spattered with pieces of my gun and pieces of shell and I have a bullet in my face and four small holes in my right shoulder.*

This VC was quite possibly the quickest to be gazetted after the action for which it was won; just one week. When it is noted that the VC for Maurice Dease, for example, whose actions at Mons made him the first VC winner of the BEF, was only gazetted three days earlier, this makes the speed of the award all the more remarkable. Dimmer also won an MC for his actions between 29 and 31 October. He went on to command a battalion and was killed at the opening of the German 1918 Spring Offensive, on 21 March, shot on horseback whilst leading his men.

Lieutenant Dimmer VC KRRC.

The French faced a certain amount of pressure on the left, but although there were alarms, nothing much came of the German action. Near the canal Moussy's force was substantially reinforced on the **13th**. An attack on the same date, which particularly hit McCracken's detachment, in the southern part of Herenthage woods, made some initial advances but the Germans were eventually removed. However, on **14 November**, German attacks on Herenthage Chateau, from the lake to the Menin Road, did result in the capture of the chateau's stables until they were ejected by the expedient of manhandling an 18 pounder gun within seventy yards of the building and shelling the occupants out. However, the Germans recaptured the stables on the 18th.

Primitive wire defences at Bayernwald (Croenart Wood).

Men of Bavarian Reserve Infantry Regiment 8 in early trenches near Wytschaete.

From **15 November** the BEF began to move out of the Salient, bringing together its two wings, which for some time now had been separated by substantial numbers of French troops; by 22 November it occupied a new line from Givenchy in the south to opposite Wytschaete in the north. The BEF was not to serve in the Salient again until February 1915.

It was an exhausted and severely tried force.

On 20 November Haig was promoted to full general for distinguished service in the field.

 In his memoirs, Oberstleutnant Fritz von Loßberg, chief of staff at Headquarters Army Group Fabeck, neatly summarised the entire First Battle of Ypres from the German perspective and the near-universal criticism of Falkenhayn's handling of it, recalling:

> *The events of 3 November demonstrated to all levels of command, up as far as Supreme Army Headquarters, that there was no way of forcing an operational success in Flanders. The necessary battle reserves and, above all, sufficient stocks of ammunition to press on with offensive operations, were simply not available. In Flanders Supreme Army Headquarters had let slip the final opportunity to gain a victory through the timely deployment of reserves released from elsewhere and the use of all the ammunition which could have been made available. This would probably have been possible had every releasable corps been made available simultaneously with Fourth Army. [These should have been] assembled on the right flank of the army, deeply echeloned and provided with sufficient ammunition, in order to smash with overwhelming force into what were then in Flanders only weak enemy forces between Diksmuide and Armentières.*
>
> *As ever, however, after the Battle of the Marne, Supreme Army Headquarters, through its slow decision making and division of the resources of the armies in the west which wore them down, always trailed behind the enemy command processes in Flanders. This made it possible for the enemy to match force with force in battle. The consequence was that the entire German Western Front was more or less condemned to positional warfare. Up to 3 November, tardy decision making by Supreme Army Headquarters led to the succession of frontal attacks by Fourth Army which cost it 49,000 men killed in action or wounded and 13,000 missing. The Sixth Army suffered about 27,000 casualties, of whom 17,250 were caused to Army Group Fabeck alone between 30 October and 3 November.*

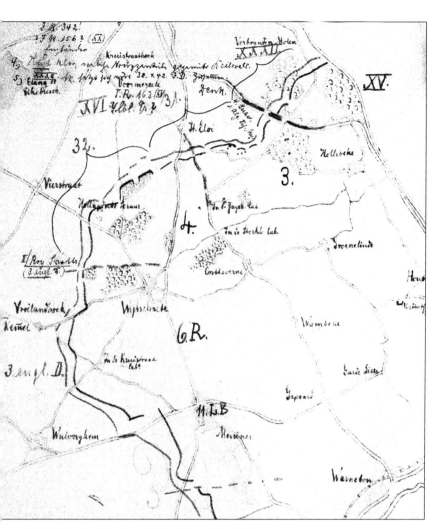

Final situation Messines Ridge November 1914.

The final reserves of ammunition were expended. The battleworthiness of the German Army of the West was considerably weakened. For the time being the German army had no capability to conduct major operations. It was absolutely essential, therefore, to break off offensive operations in the west, to adopt a defensive posture and to go at once to the aid of the Eastern Front, threatened by the weakening of the Austrians. This decision was completely obvious, but still Supreme Army Headquarters could not bring itself to take it, preferring instead to cling on to the idea of attacks in the west; this despite the

147

Men of Infantry Regiment 121 manning trenches near Messines in November.

Field Kitchen Infantry Regiment 172 Herenthage Wood.

weakened state of most of the German formations and the lack of ammunition, which all recent experience had shown might perhaps produce the odd tactical success, but had no hope of achieving anything at the operational level.

The battle may have ground to a halt with the attackers' ambitions for breakthrough thwarted, but tactically it ended with the German army securely established in dominating positions all along the Messines Ridge. It stayed there right through until 7 June 1917, when it was blown off the ridge by the simultaneous explosion of nineteen giant mines at the opening of the Battle of Messines, the precursor to the Third Battle of Ypres. This simple fact, its ability to observe virtually every single allied movement in the salient forward of Ypres, meant that it was able to cause the British huge losses in men and materiel over a thirty month period.

Between the wars in Germany the emphasis on the tragedy of Langemarck meant that the savage fighting for possession of Messines Ridge almost disappeared from popular memory. However in Bavaria the heroics of 6th Bavarian Reserve Division were never forgotten. One of their padres, Feldgeistlicher Oskar Daumiller, captured this thought later, quoting partly from the poem *Soldatenabschied* [The Soldier's Farewell] by Heinrich Lersch to make his point.

From the Bavarian perspective, the 'Spirit of Langemarck' is the 'Spirit of Wytschaete' – its hallmarks were an unparalleled disregard of the risk of death; love of and faithfulness to People, King and Fatherland; to Kaiser and Empire, in the most noble and pure sense of the words of the oath sworn on the colours. We stood together as one for our parents, wives and children; for

A battlefield cemetery at Wytschaete.

Grave of Oberleutnant Zorer Infantry Regiment 125 KIA at Messines on 5 November. This was lost in later fighting and Zorer has no known grave.

hearth and home. Our innermost conviction was, 'Germany must live, even if we have to die'. We were the physical embodiment of that rousing call to battle!

John Lucy (a corporal and later a sergeant in the 2nd Battalion Royal Irish Regiment) reflected on the final stage of the fighting of 1914, in which his battalion had been engaged from the beginning and which cost it some

340 killed, including his brother. On the evening of 19 November the battalion was relieved and prepared to leave the Salient:

The roll was being called when I joined our small party, but there was no zest in this roll call. The men stood heavily and answered listlessly. Information about dead and wounded was murmured. Our curiosity now was not for the outnumbering dead but for our few selves, and in a dazed way we inspected each other's faces, because every survivor was a phenomenon in itself. We exchanged half smiles of appreciation and silent congratulation.

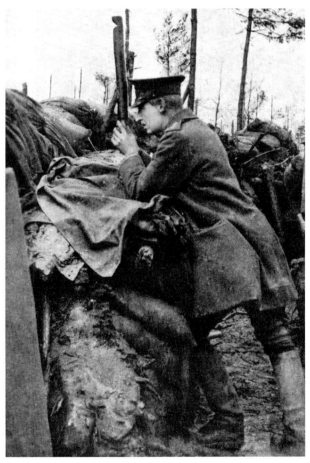

Lieutenant Horatio Fane in the Zillebeke trenches in early 1915; he died of wounds in August 1918 and is buried in Mézières Communal Cemetery, A6.

Group of Oxfordshire Hussars in the Zillebeke trenches.

Then we slouched off across the cold, barren, wintry fields, without talk, to join the main road at Hooge, and arriving there got into step once more on the hard paved road. Hooge was wrecked. South of it the Menin road from Ypres was stiff with French cavalry. They were drawn up in long lines on the west of the road with their horses' heads facing inward towards the centre of the road – massed in thousands and standing by, mounted, to check the Germans in case the British broke. They were not wanted.

The first battle for Ypres was over, and Ypres was saved.

Messines Tours

Tours 1-5 are designed to provide a detailed overview of the ground over which the lengthy battle for control of the Messines ridge and surrounding area was fought during October and November 1914. Tours 6-9 concentrate on the triangle Klein Zillebeke-Hollebeke-Kruiseke, with emphasis on the Hollebeke-Shrewsbury Forest sector.

Each tour has been designed to highlight a different aspect of the fighting and to show the dominating heights and the complexity of the topography in places. Most of the 1914 hedges have long since disappeared, but the woods have regrown more or less as they were a hundred years ago. Note, however, that they are denser and wilder than they would have been then. Many were private property and maintained for purposes of game shooting. Others, accessible to all, would have been coppiced regularly for firewood.

Because of the complexity of some of the routes, you are strongly recommended to supplement the information given here with reference to the Belgian IGNB 1:50,000 topographical map IEPER 27-28-36, usually obtainable at the In Flanders Fields Museum shop. All the roads used on the tour are marked on this map.

All the routes are suitable for car or a small minibus, but prior reconnaissance would be essential for coaches, so as to avoid low bridges or unsuitably narrow roads. Indeed, many of the roads are very narrow and so one should never be far from your car should the need arise to allow another road user by.

A note of place names
In the main text we have used the spellings as used by the British or German; in the tours section we have (we hope!) used the current version.

Tour One:

Cavalry Actions mid October 1914

(See maps on pp. 9, 15 and 21 and account on pp. 10–17.)

Start at the Les Quatre Rois crossroads **(1)**, two and a half kilometres east of Messines on the N336. Take the road ENE towards Garde Dieu, signed Komenstraat. There are excellent views to the right in the direction of Warneton and Comines. Just short of the Garde Dieu crossroads, which was the responsibility of 1 Squadron, 6th Dragoon Guards, you will see an electricity sub-station on your right. Carry straight on along the road signed Comines/Komen. The road is Le Chemin des Quatre Rois.

The next section of the tour was the responsibility of A Squadron 3rd Hussars, which established a series of troop pickets at key points. You will pass Pont Mallet Farm; then, just short of the point **(2)** where the road crosses the insignificant Kortekeerbeek, was where one of the troops was withdrawn to guard the regimental left flank, having previously been foiled

Cavalry Actions mid October 1914.

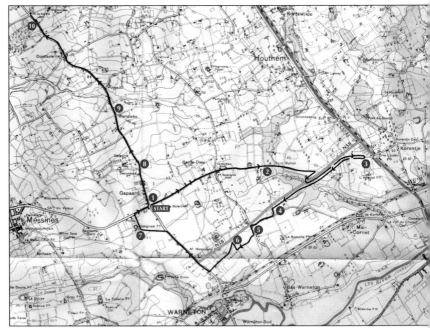

Mai Cornet and Bas Warneton churches.

in an attempt to make contact with the neighbouring regiment on the left flank at a bridge over the Ypres - Comines canal. The road bears slightly left then carry straight on at a T junction. Shortly afterwards, you will arrive in front of the N58 dual carriageway. Turn hard right at this junction, then after 100 metres take a hard left turn to an underpass which is 2.50 metres high and 2.50 metres wide and passable by a minibus. On the far side turn left, take a left fork and follow the road down as far as the old canal and the railway line **(3)**, where the picket came under fire from Comines, off on the right, and withdrew.

Retrace your steps to the railway underpass, but this time carry straight on, crossing the Kortekeerbeek once more. Moving more or less parallel to the dual carriageway, the road takes an almost 90 degree turn to the left **(4)**. This is where one of the troops was deployed in a blocking position to the south of a crossroads, which disappeared when the new road was built. Continue about one hundred metres to a junction and turn right by a house with a red tiled roof. Follow the road past a football pitch and other sporting facilities on the left. Shortly after this the road eventually turns very sharply left **(5)** where there was another troop deployed to guard a crossroads that has also disappeared. Continue to the next junction and turn right. There are good views of the churches in Warneton and Bas-Warneton. At the T junction turn right; a short distance further on at a very sharp left hand bend, which bends back towards some grey sheds, was the position of yet another troop picket of A Squadron 3rd Hussars **(6)**. Carry on past some agricultural sheds and straggly housing to a T junction.

Turn right on the N336 and pass under the dual carriageway. Drive northwest towards Gapaard, noticing a farm on your left **(7)** and a ring contour with a grey sided building, which marks the point where C Squadron 3rd Hussars was deployed then, just short of the main crossroads, were a further two troops and the regimental machine guns. From here the church at Wijtschate is very obvious.

155

Continue straight on at the crossroads, Les Quatre Rois, where you began (signed to Ypres), the road bears slightly left and on past Gapaard, marked by a few isolated buildings, where the headquarters of 3rd Hussars was based. On a slight ridge just short of the Blauepoortbeek was the location of the 3rd Hussars reserve troops and the guns of J Battery Royal Horse Artillery, which were to the east of the road and south of the Blauepoortbeek **(8)**. Continue on north. The British cavalry second position ran east - west at the crossroads just short of Wambeke **(9)**.

This tour ends at the Oosttaverne Wood Cemetery **(10)** on the left, which contains a number of 1914 burials, mainly at the rear of the cemetery. Just beyond the back wall there is a large bunker, with another about eighty metres further away, which featured in the June 1917 Battle of Messines.

The entrance to Oosttaverne Wood Cemetery with Wijtschate Church in the distance, to the right of the Cross of Sacrifice.

156

Tour Two:

The Assault of 26th Infantry Division Against Messines
30 – 31 October 1914

See also maps on pp. 69, 72, 75 77 and 83; and their accompanying text on pp. 63–82.

The tour begins at Wambeke crossroads **(1)** on the N336 by a small detached house with the number 56 on it and follows a road class 3.5 tonnes; fifty or so metres to the south on the N336 is a modern factory/warehouse set up.

Head towards Messines along what was the most northerly part of the 26th Infantry Division sector, the main effort going in slightly to the south. The road rises to a farm complex. Turn right here onto Waterputstraat then continue straight on at the junction with Kraaistraat. Carry straight on at the next junction and clear views of the ridge between Messines

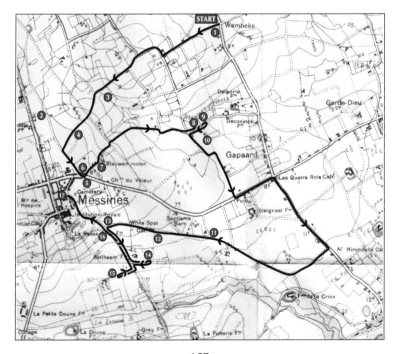

A view from 2/DG's position across to the abandoned tile factory (7), approximate site of Blauwen Molen.

and Wijtschate open up. On the ridge to your front is a prominent barn with a grey gable end. To its right is a group of yew trees planted around a cross. That is the London Scottish memorial **(2)**, which can be seen from many places on the battlefield. About 300 metres further on, pass Cabin Hill Cemetery **(3)** on your left. This relates entirely to the 1917 fighting. Turn left at the next junction with a farm complex on your immediate left. This is followed by a cross roads. Go straight on. The road rises slightly here and from the crest **(4)**, cutting across the roads and down to the left (south), were the positions of the 2nd Dragoon Guards (Queen's Bays).

The regimental history of 3/Hussars describes the move to its right at the end of a fraught day on 20 October, when the positions described in Tour 1 had been given up under German pressure (see pp 14–20). The ride to the new position (more or less from where this tour began) was described years later by an officer:

> *After all these years how that short ride comes back to one! A pitch dark night; the Colonel with a candle-lantern which kept blowing out under his cloak, escorted by two men leading his horse, intent himself upon the compass bearing, the head of the Regiment riding some five or ten yards behind him, horses stumbling along, mud up to their hocks, in half sections, and every man knowing that two hours since the Regiment had disentangled from a strong line of German infantry a short mile away on their left.*

Turn left at the T junction with Galgestraat and continue to the junction with the main N314 (Rue des Quatre Rois) and turn left again. After forty metres turn left opposite the town cemetery **(5)** onto Gapaardstraat which runs behind the slaughterhouse. Just short of this junction was the location of one of the main barricades **(6)**. As you pass the abandoned brickworks **(7)**, the site of Blauwen Molen (windmill), there is a very clear view over to the eastern approaches to Wijtschate. Go straight across at the cross roads with Langebundestraat, remaining on Gapaardstraat. Proceed past a junction on your left to a crossroads. To your front are buildings on the site of what the German sources called La Ferme **(8)**. Park near the crossroads and walk forward about one hundred metres to a point beyond La Ferme **(9)** and look left (north). Here, astride the Blauwepoortbeek, the leading companies of 1st Battalion Infantry Regiment 125 formed up prior to the assault on Messines. Rejoin your vehicle and turn south on Waterputstraat. On your left you can see a bunker **(10)** relating to the 1917 battle, which is just in a reverse slope position to an enemy advancing from the west. The assumption has to be that the divisional guns deployed more or less on the same line, sited so that their muzzles just cleared the crest line. Drive gently along the road here. It has been tarmaced, but has suffered hard usage. Drive past a rather tatty looking farm and turn left onto the main N314. This is Komenstraat. Follow it to Les Quatre Rois crossroads on the N336 and turn right, signposted to the E17, Lille, Comines and Warneton. After about nine hundred metres, keep a sharp eye open for a turn right onto a minor road adjacent to an industrial building with a stepped roof. Follow this road across open fields towards Ferme de la Croix (moved slightly north from its pre war site), where the road bears right. Continue along the road past two groups of farm buildings and just where the road begins to bear left are buildings to the right in the area known to the Germans as A la Belle Promenade **(11)** A clear view opens up of the tower in the Irish Peace Park and you are now more or less on the start line of 3rd Battalion Infantry Regiment 125 with Grenadier Regiment 119 to the south, with its left flank anchored on the Douvebeek. There are good views of Messines church up on the ridge **(12)**.

Carry on past a junction and a farm complex with a large area of greenhouses. The road bears left and at the next junction **(13)** was a

Ferme de la Croix early in the war.

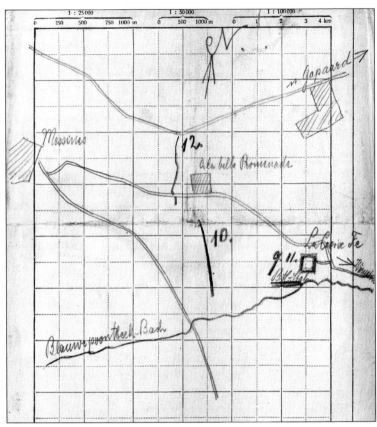

Situation Map 3rd Battalion Grenadier Regiment 119 around La Belle Promenade at 11.15 am (British time) 30 October.

View of the Irish Peace Tower and Messines Church from the east.

View to Messines and the east from Bethleem Farm West Cemetery,

barricade manned by men of 57th Rifles. Dug in a line past the south of the village were numerous slit trenches of the 57th Rifles then, running south, just to the east of the N365 between Messines and the Douvebeek, were the positions of the Royal Inniskilling Fusiliers.

Turn left and visit both the Bethleem Farm East **(14)** and West **(15)** Cemeteries; Adolf Hitler reputedly spent time in and around Bethleem Farm itself. The cemeteries offer excellent viewpoints for the battle south and east of Messines, but the graves all relate to 1917.

Retrace your steps to the junction where the 57th Rifles' barricade was and go straight into Messines. A few metres on from the junction by a calvary **(16)** is a new road running up to a house. This is probably built along the line of an old road, which ran round the south of the village in 1914. It is still possible to follow it and the subsequent rough track on foot all the way to the Messines - Ploegsteert road.

Enter Messines and park in the market square **(17)**, where this tour ends.

26th Infantry Division panoramic sketch of Messines, prior to the bombardment and assault.

View of the Abbey Church and Institute Royale pre war.

Tour Three:

A Walking Tour of Messines

See also maps on pp. 69 and 72 and text pp. 79–82.

The objective of this tour is to visit some of the key sites involved in the battle for the town of Messines itself on 31 October - 1 November 1914.

An eighteenth century view of Messines. Note the windmills - on the left now the site of Messines British Cemetery, centre, the London Scottish Memorial and on the extreme right, Blauwen Molen.

Park on the market square **(1)** in the centre of the town and head southeast along Rijselstraat/Rue de Lille towards the two Bethleem cemeteries, which are clearly signposted. When the town was reconstructed after the war, it was rebuilt more or less on the same ground plan as the original, so the older buildings occupy the same sites as their 1914 predecessors.

Just beyond the octopus crossing and the children's kindergarten **(2)**, which marks the extremity of the old town, are some modern houses and the road then bears left. There were no houses there in 1914, so the barricade here coincided more or less with the edge of the built up area and would have offered good fields of view and fire to the east.

Retrace your steps to the square, which is the point to which Leutnant Mößner and his platoon infiltrated during the night of 31 October/1 November and thereafter dominated the entire square with fire, interdicting all movement, which fragmented the defensive effort on 1 November (see pp.79–82). Leave the square at its northeastern corner on Slijtstraat/Rue des Remouleurs. Walk to the junction with Komenstraat and turn right. A major barricade **(3)** here, just level with the town cemetery, was held successively by the 11th Hussars and the 9th Lancers and assaulted by

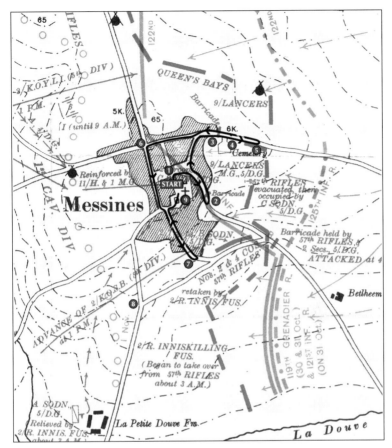

A Walking Tour of Messines

3rd Battalion Infantry Regiment 125, assisted considerably by its 1st Battalion, which outflanked the barricade to the north of the village. If you move forward to where the modern fire station (Brandweer) **(4)** stands, you are looking at the site of the 1914 brick stacks (do not confuse this site with anabandoned tile factory over to the west, which retains its prominent chimney). The main British defensive positions were forward again of that point. Walk beyond the fire station and wide views open out to the east. From a small shrine by some rough pasturage on your right the trenches of the 9th Lancers and the 57th Rifles stretched away across the fields **(5)**.

Walk back along Komenstraat past the Rue des Remouleurs on what is now Steenstraat (on one side and Komenstraat on the other!). A shop on this street sells sandwiches.

Carry on to the crossroads with the main N365 and turn left. This junction **(6)** was held by C & D Squadrons of 11/Hussars. Continue down the street, which was the site of intense fighting involving the use of

The crossroads defended by 11/Hussars.

manhandled German artillery pieces at point blank range, past the market square to the point where the main road bears off 90 degrees to the right.

Carry straight on to the southern tip of the village along Daalstraat. The tarmac road finishes by a modern grey house **(7)**, but a rough track leads down into the low ground in the direction of the Douvebeek. This is the area of the barricade manned by 5th Dragoon Guards. From this point it is clear why it was established here, because the fields of fire open up in all directions. It is possible to see well beyond Bethleem Cemetery West to the south east, whilst off to the west is a clear view of the Irish Peace Park **(8)**, which marks roughly the line, running north, where the men of Infantry Regiment 125 dug in having captured the village. It is possible to go forward along a rough track to view the line held by the Royal Inniskilling Fusiliers (which was also the attack sector of Grenadier Regiment 119), then to complete a circuit of the village to the left or right, but this is likely to be a muddy proposition in anything but dry weather.

Walk now to the church **(9)**, which is still impressive, but a shadow of its former glory. Stones let into the ground

Messines Abbey Church; the Institute Royale ran along the right hand side of the street.

164

give an indication of its original dimensions and those of the adjoining Institute Royale. Within the church are information boards, displaying photographs of the village before, during and after the war, whilst the crypt is open to all and is worth a visit. Buried in the crypt is St Adèle of France (feast day on 8 September, for those who might be interested). She died in 1079, but not before seeing her son in law, William the Conqueror, crowned King of England. She was the foundress of what became a prestigious abbey, until it was dissolved in the Josephite reforms of the late eighteenth century. The underground space was also used by the regimental command post of Bavarian Reserve Infantry Regiment 16 at one point in 1914. Hence Adolf Hitler himself must have sheltered here, in between carrying messages forward to the various battalions of the regiment.

From the church, head back to the market square along Kortemooiestraat. The tour ends back at your car on the square.

The Institution (sometimes called the Institute) Royale.

165

Tour Four:

Operations West of Messines
2 – 10 November

See also map on p. 77 and text pp. 75–76 and 103–105.

Leave Messines on the N314 in the direction of Wulvergem.

Just by the new Vrededorp **(1)** on the left is a memorial plaque to the French Chasseurs d'Afrique, who were deployed here in late 1914, once the British army left Stop at Messines Ridge British cemetery **(2)**, which was the limit of exploitation of Infantry Regiment 125 on 1 November 1914.

The cemetery offers good views towards the British rear positions at

Chasseurs d'Afrique Memorial.

Operations West of Messines.

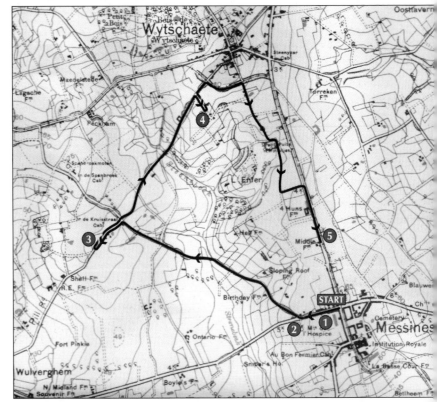

View towards Nieuwkerke (left) and Wulvergem (right).

Messines and what was then to prove to be the British line for many months after the fighting had settled down in this area. Wulvergem is down in the dip, Neuve Eglise (Nieuwkerke) on the high ground beyond. The road from Wulvergem was an approach road for the British infantry reinforcements that were rushed forwards on 31 October.

The Cross of Sacrifice (surrounded by a New Zealand Memorial to the Missing) stands on the site of the mill that belonged to the Institution Royale and previously to that to the Abbey.

This is a concentration cemetery. There are few identified 1914 casualties buried here and only two from the Messines fighting: Captain Payne Gallwcy (II F 8) was on leave when war broke out and he was seconded from his regiment, 21st (Empress of India) Lancers, to 9/ Lancers. He was killed on 30 October (31 October, according to other sources), almost certainly in the defence of Messines. Private Francis Macdonald (V D 2), also 21/Lancers but attached to 9/Lancers, was killed on 31 October. It seems strange that there should be two from the 21st serving with 9/Lancers: idle speculation offers the possibility that Macdonald was Galway's orderly. The only other identified 1914 casualty is Private Joseph Leighton, 6/DG (VI A 25), who died on 13 November.

From here take the minor road leading northwest towards Spanbroekmolen. Pass a road junction with a road leading off to the right and a minor crossroads before reaching Kruisstraathoek. Turn left here

he Cross of Sacrifice on the site of the old windmill.

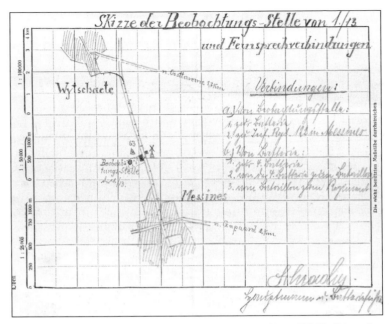

Location of OP 1st Battery Field Artillery Regiment 13 on Hill 63, November 1914. The sketch includes details of all telephone links to the battery, battalion and regiment. Situated near the London Scottish Memorial.

and drive up to the crest of the hill **(3)** where two of the Kruisstraat mines were blown in 1917. From this position there is an excellent view back towards Messines and the ground across which the formations of the Pomeranian 3rd Infantry Division fought as they advanced the line towards Spanbroekmolen in pursuit of the elusive breakthrough.

Retrace your route to Kruisstraathoek and go straight on at the crossroads towards Wijtschate. The church is obvious, so continue to head towards it. About 500 metres short of Wijtschate a road leads to the right to the summit of Hill 77.5 **(4)**. It is worth a short diversion to benefit from the German viewpoint for much of the war at the top, near a farm; there is a helpful annotated panoramic photograph mounted on a plinth. The London Scottish moved near here, slightly to the east, in their advance to the fighting line on 31 October

Just as you enter the village, immediately after the Wijtschate sign, take a turn to the right onto Guido Gezellestraat then, after about 100 metres, turn right again onto Schoolstraat, heading just east of south past an electricity sub-station and a prominent red and white radio mast on your left. Continue straight on at a crossroads and on where the road jinks left then right to a sharp turn to the left a short distance from the N365 Wijtschate - Messines road. Turn right onto the main road (Ieperstraat) and the tour ends at the memorial to the London Scottish **(5)** on the left hand side of the road.

The London Scottish Memorial. The memorial was unveiled by King Albert
I of the Belgians in May 1924, in the presence of the regiment's honorary
colonel, since 1919, Earl Haig, and members of the London Scottish, past
and present. King Albert flew himself to the ceremony, landing in the fields
nearby.

The memorial is sited close to or on the foundations of a windmill. With
the distinctive trees, on high ground, it is visible from as far away as
Kruiseke. It stands on the right of the London Scottish line, which was about
100 metres forward of it, to the east.

Tour Five:

A Loop Around Wijtschate

See also maps on pp. 75, 77, 96, 109, 110 and 111 and text pp. 95–116.

This tour is intended to familiarise you with the complex terrain around Wijtschate.

    Start at the London Scottish Memorial and drive north along the N365, until you see a sign for Hollebeke 5, which is also signed to Somer Farm Cemetery **(1)**. Turn right and drive past the cemetery. It is worth pausing here to look at the ground to the east of the ridge where much of the fighting took place. A little further on a road leads off to the right towards a farm. More or less at this point was a forward position of the 57th Rifles **(2)**. Further forward a pair of bunkers may be seen to the south of Oosttaverne Wood Cemetery. These relate to the 1917 battle.

A Loop around Wijtschate.

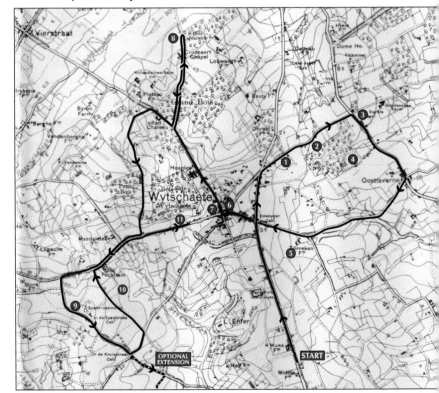

170

Continue to the N336 main road and turn right onto Rijselstraat. Directly opposite is the memorial to the British 19th (Western) Division **(3)**. Carry on past the cemetery and continue down to the Oosttaverne crossroads, passing under a pylon line and turn right by a house with a cream coloured wall, heading back towards Wijtschate.

Wijtschate comes into view on the right and Messines directly to your front. About one kilometre along this road, it bears to the right and north of the road can be seen a prominent wood **(4)**. This occupies part of the site of Rondell Wood/Oosttaverne Wood, which was much more extensive in 1914 than it is today, when its north eastern tip reached almost to Oosttaverne Wood Cemetery. It is more or less certain that the clash between Bavarian Reserve Infantry Regiments 17 and 21 occurred when leading elements of the latter exited the western edge of the wood during the early morning of 1 November and mistook the men of Bavarian Reserve Infantry Regiment 17 for British troops.

Straight on past a turn to the left, where the road swings to the right, and Torreken Farm Cemetery Number 1 **(5)** can be seen off to the left. During the battle for Wijtschate, Headquarters 12 Bavarian Reserve Brigade, commanded by Generalmajor Kiefhaber, was based here.

It was also the location of a brave action on 4 November 1914 by Unteroffizier Georg Fuchs of Reserve Telephone Detachment 6, attached to the brigade. That morning he was in charge of a line laying party, which had been tasked with connecting Oosttaverne and 12 Bavarian Reserve Brigade. On approaching Torreken Farm, he witnessed a panicky retreat by soldiers, horses and wagons from Wijtschate, following a French attack. Having largely failed to check the withdrawal by shouting orders at the passing soldiers, he threatened to shoot anyone who attempted to continue to the rear. He succeeded eventually in gathering a party of about fifty around him, calming and rallying them, then led them forward through a torrent of French artillery and small arms fire to the northeast tip of the village, where they arrived in the nick of time to prevent a serious situation becoming a crisis. History does not record if he then returned to laying line, but he was awarded an immediate Bavarian Silver Medal for Bravery.

At the junction with the main N365 turn left, then fork to the left after one hundred metres, along a road signed to Torreken Farm Cemetery. Although the cemetery has no connection with 1914 it is worth visiting (despite the complex series of gates!) because it offers excellent views over the approaches to Wijtschate from the east.

Retrace your steps to the main road, turn right, then first left along Staanijzerstraat into the centre of Wijtschate to the square by the church. On the square is a general grocery store **(6)** that sells a limited range of food and drinks. Go round the square on its northern side and head north out of the village, leaving the church on your right. Here you will see a sign to Bayernwald and De Croonaert and a bronze statue of a miner **(7)**, which is linked to a later phase of operations in the area.

On your left you will see a modern gymnasium built on the site of what

171

Wijtschate Square.

was known during the war as a hospice. This is a misnomer, certainly in a modern context. It was an agricultural training establishment, certainly with orphans in mind, but there were also paying pupils (a long planned project which came to fruition in 1911, only to be destroyed a few years later), which is mentioned in several contemporary accounts. The same benefactor left money for a similar establishment in Loker (Locre Hospice during the war), for orphan girls for training in domestic skills.

Eventually the road bends to the left and the road to Bayernwald forks off to the right. If you wish to visit the trenches of Bayernwald **(8)**, you must contact the tourist office in Kemmel (Tel: 0032 257 450 455 or visit the website: www. heuvelland.be) in order to receive the combination of the lock on the gate.

Originally known as the Beilformiger Wald [hatchet-shaped wood], the area was christened after the successful attack on it between 15 and 17 November by the formations of 12 Bavarian Reserve Brigade, 6th Bavarian Reserve Division, under the command of Oberstleutnant Petz of Bavarian Reserve Infantry Regiment 17. This was the final piece of vital ground on this part of the ridge. From the northern tip of Bayernwald it is possible to see all the way to Ypres, demonstrating what a key dominating position this was.

The attack on the *Beilformigerwald*, later to be known as *Bayernwald*, was launched at 8.00 am (UK time) on 15 November. Bavarian Reserve Infantry Regiments 16 and 17 went forward together, but the initial assault was shot to a standstill in a hail of small arms fire. Oberstleutnant Engelhardt, who had assumed command after the death of Oberst List during the earlier attack on Geluveld, sought to renew the assault, but a second effort at about 2.30 pm enjoyed no greater success. Impatient to move closer and rally his men for a further effort, Engelhardt decided to go forward and take personal charge of the operation. Accompanied by two of his runners - Adolf Hitler and a second man named Bachmann - he moved under cover of a sunken road to the edge of the wood and climbed up the bank to where he could get a clear view of proceedings. It nearly cost him his life. Concentrating on his study of the ground, he failed to note a sudden burst of rifle and machine gun fire directed at him. Spotting the extreme danger, Hitler and Bachman launched themselves at him and dragged him into cover in a nearby hole in the ground, allegedly shouting that the regiment could ill afford to lose a second commander so soon. Be that as it may, Engelhardt silently shook both men by the hand in thanks for their quick-witted action. It did not prolong his life for long, however, because he was shot and killed two days later in similar circumstances when the wood for which so much Bavarian blood had been spilled was finally secured and named *Bayernwald* in their honour. It was for actions such as this that Adolf Hitler was awarded the Iron Cross Second Class. The Germans regarded this as the final significant episode of the First Battle of Ypres.

After its capture there were no more attacks of anything other than local significance throughout the coming winter. Within forty eight hours of this success, Bavarian Reserve Infantry Regiment 16 (List) lost its second commander in quick succession when Phillip Engelhardt was hit in the brachial artery of his left arm but survived, despite the loss of blood. *Ich wollte nur meinem Vaterlande dienen* [I wished only to serve my country] were his parting words.

Retrace your steps back to the main road and turn hard right onto Vierstraat. This was the major route used by the French army to reinforce and resupply their positions to the west of Wijtschate; and where they brought up reinforcements in the struggle for the village. Take the first left turn, which drops down into low ground and continues to wind forward, passing wooded areas, until you arrive at a T junction with a row of modern houses to your front. Turn right at this point. Carry straight on past a road to the right and the road up to Spanbroekmolen Cemetery, taking the next left turn, which is signed to Lone Tree Cemetery. Drive up the hill past a turning to the right, bear left at a fork and you arrive at

Spanbroek Molen before the war.

Spanbroekmolen Pool of Peace **(9).** There is a small layby just before the crater, on the left; and nearby some annotated panorama panels. Walk around the crater to take advantage of the views from this prominent height, especially on its eastern side; British artillery was situated on the slight reverse slope to the north during the fighting for Messines Ridge; it was to this area that the British line withdrew, reinforced by a significant deployment of French troops.

Continue past Lone Tree Cemetery and proceed to the Kruisstraathoek crossroads, where you turn left.

Messines Church (left of centre) and the Irish Peace Tower (right of centre) from the east side of the crater

Optional Tour Extension:

Christmas Truce 1914

At the crossroads continue straight on, as if for Messines Ridge British Cemetery. After a hundred metres or so take the first right turn (Katteputstraat) and then turn right again, on to Kortestraat and also signed for Mitelweg Hoeve, following this road around as it makes a sharp left turn, passing a farm on your right (Mittel Ferme to the Germans). This road runs parallel with the post Ypres line, on the right. Continue to the N314, turn left and take the next left, which will take you past Back Ferme,

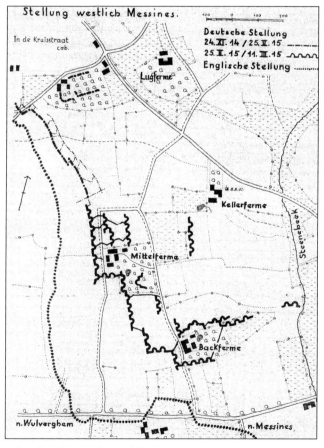

A map showing the positions of Bavarian Reserve Infantry Regiment 16.

to the British Ontario Farm, scene of one of the mines fired on 7th June: this one left no crater. It was in this area, between and in front of the farms, that there was a local truce at Christmas 1914.

This occurred in the sector of Bavarian Reserve Infantry Regiment 16, which ran from a point about one kilometre west of Messines, north past two farms, known as Back Ferme and Mittel Ferme (which still exist under Flemish names today) to Kruisstraathoek. A couple of days previously there had been an instance of Bavarian Reserve Infantry Regiment 17 permitting the British troops opposite to bury their dead forward of their positions without being disturbed. This then developed into a more general ceasefire, with soldiers of both sides meeting in No Man's Land on Christmas Day to exchange cigarettes and souvenirs with one another. On the British side, the troops involved during the next few days were from 14 and 15 Brigade, 5th Division, with 1/Norfolk, 2/Manchester and 1/Devonshire being mentioned specifically in the German account. Max Herold, 8th Company Bavarian Reserve Infantry Regiment 16, received and kept some postcards and photographs,

A pre war image of a despatch rid from 2nd Manchesters, given to Max Herold, 8th Company Bavaria Reserve Infantry Regiment 16, an inscribed, 'I wish you a very Happ Christmas!'

inscribed with greetings such as, 'Wishing you a very Happy Christmas and a speedy end to the war', whilst another man, Josef Wenzel, who was killed later in the war whilst on flying duties in May 1917, wrote home to his parents to describe his astonishment at what happened:

What I am about to tell you must seem almost beyond belief, but is the absolute truth. At 4.00am on 26 December we entered the trenches on a clear starry night. Everything was frozen hard and we should have been seen. I expected to come under heavy fire, but to my astonishment there was no firing. The men we relieved explained to us that they had swapped things with the British and I should not have believed it, had I not found proof in the form of some English cigarettes in my dugout, which I much enjoyed. Hardly had day dawned than the British began to wave to us and our men returned the gestures. Gradually they left their trenches. Our men took out a Christmas tree complete with candles, which they placed on a wall and lit up. They then rang bells and everyone moved out of their trenches; nobody thought of opening fire. That which only hours ago I should have thought was nonsense I now saw with my own eyes. A British soldier, who was then joined by a second man, came from our left and crossed more than halfway into No Man's Land, where they met up with our men. British and Bavarians, previously the worst of enemies, stood there shaking hands and exchanging items. The one star still in the sky above them was regarded by the men as a special sign from Heaven. Increasingly more and more joined in all along the line, shaking hands and swapping souvenirs. More than half of my platoon went out.

Because I wanted to take a closer look at these chaps and obtain a souvenir, I moved towards a group of them. Immediately one came up to me, shook my hand and gave me some cigarettes; another gave me a handkerchief, a third signed his name on a field postcard and a fourth wrote his address in my notebook. Everyone mingled and conversed to the best of their ability. One British soldier played the mouth organ of a German comrade, some danced around, whilst others took great pride in trying on the German helmets. One of our man placed a Christmas tree in the middle, pulled out a box of matches from his pocket and in no time the tree was lit up. The British sang a Christmas carol and we followed this with 'Silent Night, Holy Night'. It was a moving moment; between the trenches stood the most hated and bitter enemies and sang Christmas carols. All my life I shall never forget the sight ... Christmas 1914 will be completely unforgettable.

From here, continue northwards on this road; there are superb views along the length of Messines Ridge. Pass the junction where you turned left for Mittel Ferme; at the T junction turn left, which will bring you back to the Kruisstraat crossroads. At this point turn right, heading towards Wijtschate.

End of Optional Tour Extension.

All the ground to the west of Messines is clearly visible from here and note all the dips and dead ground in this area, which played a significant role in the fighting here. As the road rises, take the first left turning onto Scheerstraat. Spanbroekmolen crater is very obvious off to the left. It is possible to park a car or minibus off the road and visit Spanbroekmolen Cemetery down to the right **(10)**. It has no 1914 significance, except that it does offer good views over the ground to the west of Wijtschate, in particular of the ground of the Lincolns and Northumberland Fusiliers as they attempted to retrieve the situation in Wijtschate in the early hours of 1 November, with consequent heavy losses. Here on the left, to the rear of the rising ground and to the right of the Spanbroekmolen crater, is where British gun lines were in 1914.

At the T junction turn right onto Wijtschatestraat. Follow the road all the way in to Wijtschate, pausing at Wytschaete Military Cemetery **(11)**,

Wytschaete Military Cemetery.

which contains a few known First Ypres burials – a couple from the Lincolns, a couple of cavalrymen and two London Scottish: Private Charles Wallace (III B 44) and Lance Corporal Eric Chapman (III B 45). Of the 113 London Scottish in the CWGC records for the whole of the period of the battle, only these two, one buried at Bedford House, one who died of wounds as a Prisoner of War and is buried in Lille South, a few killed away from the Salient and a few who died of wounds, in total sixteen, have a known grave. This leaves all the others, ninety seven of them, commemorated on the Menin Gate.

The tour ends back in the centre of Wijtschate.

Tour Six:

The Kruiseke-Zandvoorde Area

See also maps on pp. 39, 44, 50 and 53 and text pp. 39–51.

From the junction of the N8 Menin Road and the N 303, drive south along the latter for 500 metres to a minor cross roads and turn right (west) onto Dornkapellestraat. Follow the road round, taking the left turn at a fork with Geluveld sign next to it and a low white walled building to your left **(1)**. [If you had carried straight on, some two hundred metres in the fields to the right was where Lieutenant James Brooke performed the heroic actions on 29 October that gained him a posthumous VC.] You are heading in the general area of Zandvoorde and the views open up. It is now clear that Zandvoorde sits on a distinct rise and that, therefore, it was of tactical importance to both sides. It was put into all round defence by the British

The Kruiseke - Zandvoorde area .

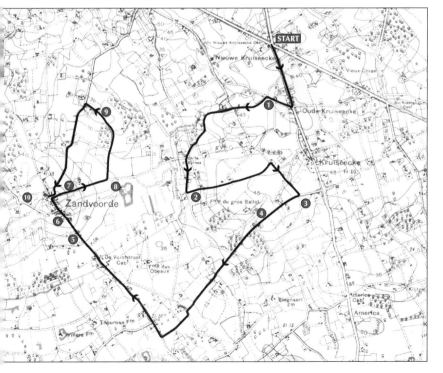

army, with emphasis on the northern and eastern sides. Carry straight on along Dornkapellestraat past three successive turnings to the right then take a tight turn to the left marked 43 LF 6 Vlanderen Fiets Route. This is Nieuwe Zoetenstraat. As it climbs towards Kruiseke there is a good view over to Geluveld on the left **(2)**. It is worth pulling in (carefully!) towards the crest of the hill and taking in the views behind you to the west. As you approach Kruiseke the road turns sharply right onto Tabakstraat. There is a small vineyard at this point. Carry on through a sports complex to a cross roads with a grey coloured modern house on your left. Find a parking place and walk forward to examine the ground to the south of the village **(3)**, defended by elements of 20 Brigade, 7th Division.

Despite the fact that Kruiseke is naturally a fairly strong position, it ultimately fell on 26 October, after a period of pressure, to a mixed German force, which, in addition to some Jägers, mainly comprised the dismounted elements of 22 and 25 Cavalry Brigades of the German 3rd Cavalry Division. These included Dragoner Regiment 5, Husaren Regiment 14, Garde-Dragoner Regiment 23 and Leib-Dragoner Regiment 24. A member of the last named recalled:

> *At 11.00 am on 26 October, the British began to leave their front line trenches. When our troopers saw this, without waiting for orders, they rushed forward from their inadequate dug outs under the command of Hauptmann Riedesel Freiherr zu Eisenbach, determined to take revenge on an enemy who had inflicted such heavy losses upon them. Despite being swept at times by machine gun fire, they charged into the British trenches. Before the British knew what was happening and were able to defend themselves [we were amongst them]. A few showed signs of attempting to resist so it was necessary to go in with lead and rifle butts to demonstrate that further resistance was useless. Encouraged, the dragoons pressed on into the narrow trenches and took one hundred prisoners.*
>
> *The Royal Scotch Guards [sic.] were astonished at the sight of our spurs and one officer, realising that their trenches had fallen to the cavalry, attempted suicide. The assault was continued on beyond these trenches towards Kruiseke, where a great many of the enemy were taken prisoner. Orders were then given to halt any further advance. The edges of the village were all picketed and once initial duties were complete, the dragoons helped themselves to captured British preserved rations and cigarettes.*

This was quite an achievement for the German cavalry, who were nowhere near as well equipped for this style of fighting as their British counterparts. Discussing the issue, Rittmeister von Boddien of the élite Gardes du Corps, which was deployed over towards Messines, pointed out:

At that time the cavalry (especially the Gardes du Corps, with their high hussar's riding boots, complete with spurs, which frequently caught in barbed wire) were extremely badly equipped for the infantry battle. Because no side arms were available and the carbines were not designed to take a bayonet, lances had to be taken into the forward battle area, so as to have available a close quarter weapon. Even worse was the fact that the men had no spades and had to dig in with bare hands and spoons. Then, in order to get in a final jibe at the Allies, Boddien continued: *It really is a miracle and an indication of how poor the enemies' marksmanship training was that during all these battles hardly any casualties were caused by small arms fire; even those resulting from artillery fire were very few.*

Return to your vehicle and turn right, driving southwest through Hoge Bossen (High Wood). From the edge of the wood **(4)**, you can see all the way to the Messines Ridge and even at this range to locate the London Scottish memorial, over five miles away.

Zandvoorde church on the right, standing on high ground. On the left Wijtschaete Church is just visible, with the mass of Kemmel Hill to its right.

Descend the hill, noting how open the ground is to your right, whilst off to the left the church tower in Ten Brielen comes into view. Jink left and right past some large farm buildings and then, at a T junction with the Zandvoorde - Ten Brielen road, turn right onto the Rue de Zandvoorde/Zandvoordestraat. On 30 October, Zandvoorde was defended by 7 Cavalry Brigade and was attacked directly by Infantry Regiment 172 on the left of the road and a Bavarian Jäger Battalion on the right. General der Kavallerie Georg von der Marwitz, who had been given responsibility for all cavalry operations in the area, was glad to hand over responsibility for the attack to the infantry. Writing home to his wife the a few days previously, he noted:

I passed a dull day behind the long, over-extended front. I am currently in command of no fewer than eight cavalry divisions, but their deployment could hardly be more different than when on exercise at Döberitz. The entire countryside here is one mass of small enclosed fields and hedges reinforced with wire. How are we meant to attack through that?! The enemy exploits its potential skilfully, firing from inside houses and trenches, which they have dug extremely rapidly. Just recently we were in the same situation when we had a long line to defend. The attackers launched their assaults in vain and had no success.

An elaborate German bunker dating from 1916 is on your right **(5)** as you enter the village. It is well worth a visit and there is an illuminating information plaque next to it. Look to your left as you continue towards the village centre.

On your left and opposite a shrine is a gate surrounded by white stone walls. This is entrance the approach to the Household Cavalry memorial **(6).**

Household Cavalry Memorial and Plaque.

Lord Worsley.

Find a parking space (there is usually plenty of space by the shrine) and visit the memorial; this was unveiled by Field Marshal Haig, then Colonel of the Blues, in 1924 (he also happened to be Lady Apsley's brother in law). It stands on the spot where the body of 27 year old Lord Worsley, then in C Squadron of the RHG, commanding the machine gun section, was first buried (now in Ypres Town Cemetery Extension, II D 4) and the ground was purchased by his widow, Lady Apsley. It commemorates the men of 1 and 2 Life Guards and the Royal Horse Guards who fell in 1914 – 234 from the Life Guards and sixty two from the RHG. Once more there are views across to Messines to the south west. If you walk back down the road a short distance and look east, you can see all the way back to Kruiseke.

Return to your car and carry on into the centre of the village. Just short of the church look for the sign to Zantvoorde Cemetery and turn right. Stop at the cemetery **(7)**, which contains numerous burials relating to 1914.

Zantvoorde British Cemetery.

The spelling is as above – from somewhere a 't' has come in; it does not seem to have been spelt that way even in 1914. This cemetery provides commanding views of much of the battlefield south of the Menin Road – indeed, almost the whole length of the Menin Road that was engulfed by the fighting at First Ypres, from Geluwe to Herenthage Wood, can be seen from the rear wall. From the area of the Cross of Sacrifice one can see the church in Kruiseke and the western part of the spur on which that village is built, as well as the church spires in Comines and Tenbrielen.

This a large cemetery, created after the war by bringing in small plots, isolated graves and a number from German cemeteries. Over a hundred of those identified – about 20% - are casualties of First Ypres, though a number of these are in reality a commemoration, as their graves could not be identified individually when they were brought in from Wervicq Road German Cemetery and Kruiseecke (sic) German Cemetery. These are to be found in a rectangular arrangement of headstones at the northern end of the cemetery.

Amongst the officers buried here are Henry Crighton of the Royal Horse Guards, kia on 31 October 1914 (V B 11). Captain Clement Ransford, 1/S Staffs, aged 32, is buried in VI J 19. Lieutenant Colonel Beauchamp Pell, the Queen's Royal Regiment (West Surrey) is in II F 1. He died on 4 November, fatally wounded when his battalion was all but destroyed in the defence of the southern approaches to Gheluvelt. His epitaph comes from Psalm 48, v 14. Major Humphrey St Leger Stuckley commanded the King's Company of 1/Grenadier Guards. Philip van Neck, also

Lieutenant Colonel BT Pell DSO.

183

1/Grenadier, was killed on 26 October, aged 27 (V H 14). His brother, Charles van Neck, was killed on 20 October whilst serving with 1/Northumberland Fusiliers. He now rests in Cabaret Rouge (to the north of Arras, a major concentration cemetery for casualties from all over the British part of the Western Front), XVI B 17. Lieutenant (but, note, his rank is given as captain on the headstone) Brooke, 2/Gordons, was killed on 29 October (VI E 2). A Sword of Honour winner at Sandhurst, he was 30 when he fell; he was subsequently awarded a posthumous VC. On his headstone (his epitaph is another biblical one, this time from St Paul) he is given the rank of captain, which is correct; in fact he was promoted on 1 September, but the notification of this did not arrive until after his death.

In recent years the Commission has provided useful information plaques in many of its cemeteries and memorials, and this is the case here. These often include relevant contemporary photographs, such as this one of members of the Scot Guards resting at Gheluveld in October 1914.

Carry on down the slope to a crossroads and turn left. Zandvoorde Chateau – in reality a good sized farm, destroyed during the war – was

located just to the south east of this crossroads **(8)**. To the right you can see up the sloping ground towards Kruiseke; the Royal Welch Fusiliers were all but destroyed in the fighting here on 30 October, holding a very over extended position around the chateau area and for a considerable distance to its left and right.

After a wood on your left, there are good views on the high ground towards Geluveld **(9)**. At the Geluveld - Zandvoorde road turn left. Pause at the church in Zandvoorde, which carries plaques describing its reconstruction **(10)**. In its churchyard there are buried four casualties of 10/Hussars, all four killed on 26 October 1914, amongst them Captain Sir Frank Stanley Day and Lieutenant Christopher Turnor. The church, which is usually open during working hours, has a fine stained glass window erected by Turnor's family in memory of him. There are a few small shops in Zandvoorde as well as at least one bar.

Tour Seven:

Shrewsbury Forest and Surrounding Area

.

See also, eg, maps on pp 118, 125, 138 and text pp 116-118 and 126 – 134.

This tour is designed to show the complexity of the ground and the dense nature of the wooded area between Zandvoorde and Zillebeke, where command and control was extremely difficult for both attacker and defender.

From Zandvoorde church **(START)** leave the Gildenhof pub on your left and head along the road signposted to Ieper to the northern tip of the village, where the main road swings to the left. Carry straight on at this point down a minor road signposted to Gasthuisbossen. Watch out for traffic joining from the right. There are good views towards Geluveld to

Shrewsbury Forest and surrounding area.

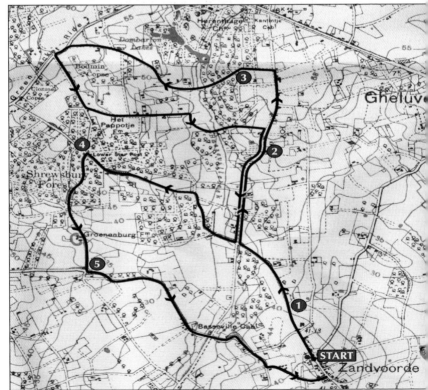

the right **(1)**, whilst looming up on your left is the great mass of Shrewsbury Forest (Groenenburgbos) and further across on the left Messines is once more clearly visible. At a crossroads turn right onto Waterstraat and drive north towards Veldhoek. The road jinks right (there is a German bunker over on the left here) then left again. On your right there is a farm entrance **(2)** where you have some space to pull over and view the close countryside to the west. Although much of the hedging has gone, there is still a reasonable impression of the close nature of the countryside; whilst the distinct shape of Hollebeke Church is visible to the west.

Continue past a turning to the left and two to the right, before turning left at a crossroads onto Herenthagestraat. Agricultural buildings with four pale blue silos are on your right. Where the road bears left, there is a 1982 private memorial to a Gunner Wheeler **(3)**, who was wounded here on 1 July 1916, but who lived until 1982; his ashes were scattered in Bedford House Cemetery. As you drop into low undulating ground there are still numerous small enclosures and hedges and thick woods either side; all rather evocative of the situation in 1914. Carry straight on at a minor junction, heading towards the road to Zillebeke. Sanctuary Wood looms up to your front at this point. Turn left onto the main road, known during the war as Green Jacket Drive, then a hundred metres further on left again onto Kranenburgstraat. Down to the south is Shrewsbury Forest. At the northern tip of the wood, turn left at a crossroads onto Passendaleveldstraat. Note the density of the woods in this area. The thickness of the trees and much reduced visibility because of the thick undergrowth had a marked effect on the fighting in this area. Fritz Grieshammer, of 8th Company Infantry Regiment 172, later given a reserve commission as a leutnant, arrived with a party of reinforcements when the fighting for this wooded area was at its height. He has provided us with highly atmospheric account of the confused situation in which he found himself:

> The area was heavily wooded. We stumbled over many fallen trees, then arrived in an open area. We doubled forward and somebody collapsed immediately, shot through the stomach from a flank. We ran for our lives to a trench and, luckily, got there. From there, ducking low, we headed off to the right as British bullets whistled past. One of us was ordered to take a message to the rear. He leapt up out of the trench, took what he thought was cover behind a tree and glanced at the enemy. There was a shot and he fell down moaning. The poor lad then made his way back to us and lay at my feet, shot through the arm. I tore off his sleeve, bandaged him up and then prepared to move. An oberleutnant was determined to lead us forward. He jumped up out of the trench and fell to the ground, hit by three bullets in the upper thigh, stomach and foot. His batman rushed to his side as he lay still on the ground. We continued, leaderless, reaching a shot up wood at the cost of further casualties. We reorganised. Volunteers forward! Are there enemy trenches to our front? I crept forward and, thank heavens, the trench was occupied by Germans. Right, keep going! I carried on to the front line trench and continued further, flat on my stomach. I was filled with determination. The British were a mere thirty metres further forward … night fell, it was impossible for us to launch an attack; we were too weak. With this [awful] weather, enormous casualties (our three companies were down to a total of 100 men) in this terrain, an assault was impossible. Suddenly there were stirrings in the wood behind us. Our forces were pulling back. '172nd, rally on the left!' … I took the lead; it was complete chaos. I could not locate anyone. We followed our noses and eventually came across the Feldwebel. I then set about pulling together anyone wandering aimlessly round the wood …

The road bends sharply round at a right angle to the right, then left once more at another junction where there is a view of Zandvoorde church in the distance. Drop down across the minor Bassevillebeek and up to a T junction. Turn right, back on to Waterstraat. Head down the hill, noting the size of Shrewsbury Forest. Continue down to a line of poplar trees on the right, just before a sharp turn to the right at a crossroads (the one which you passed earlier, coming from Zandvoorde) onto Vijfwegenstraat) and head towards the wood. Enter the wood. When you get to centre of the wood at Lower Star Post **(4)**, turn left onto Kranenburgstraat, signposted Hollebeke 4.4 km. It is possible to pull off the road at Lower Star Post and it might be an appropriate time to look at the maps and the accounts of the complex fighting in the wooded areas around here: see pp for maps and text. The situation was often perilous for the British (and the French who came to their assistance); whilst it was not pleasant at all for the Germans, particularly as the weather deteriorated as November progressed.

There is a minor crossroads at the edge of the wood. Carry straight on here, remaining on Kranenburgstraat. Carry on up the hill. There is a calvary to your front at a T junction on the road to Zandvoorde.

Turn left onto Zillebekestraat. This is a major road for the area, carrying high speed traffic. The tour ends at Zandvoorde church.

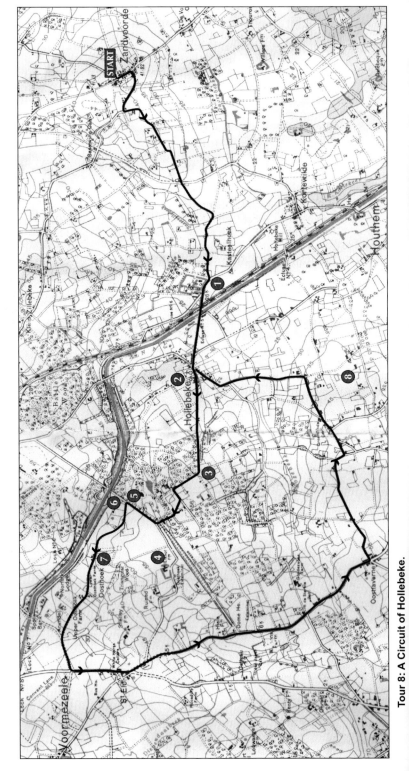

Tour 8: A Circuit of Hollebeke.

Tour Eight:

Circuit of Hollebeke

See also maps on pp. 39, 44, 87 and 96 and text pp. 40–41 and 84–88.

This tour is designed to highlight the battles for Hollebeke and, in particular, two nearby chateaux - now disappeared.

From the church at Zandvoorde head south on the road towards Werwik and Ten Brielen; whilst still within the village, turn right onto Houtemstraat, signed to Houtem and Hollebeke. This road runs west out of Zandvoorde along a spur and past the new Holland agricultural centre. There are excellent views out to Wijtschate, Hollebeke church and Messines. Turn right onto a minor road, signed Hollebeke Golf, then immediately left onto Hollebekestraat. At Kasteelhoek bear left at a fork, heading towards Hollebeke church. At a junction with a major road, bear right along

The large and distinctive Hollebeke Church.

Kortewildestraat. Go straight on at a fork, and head for an underpass under the railway (maximum headroom 2.68 metres!). There is a bunker embedded in the embankment to the left of the railway bridge. On your

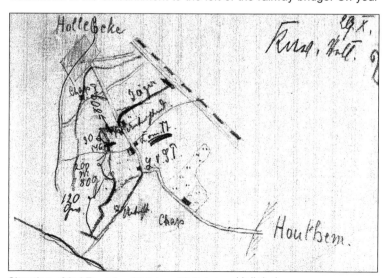

Situation of 3rd Bavarian Division, 29 October, Hollebeke

right is an extensive area of polytunnels called 't Drevehof. This is more or less on the site of Hollebeke Chateau **(1)**, captured by the regiments of 4th Bavarian Infantry Division and later destroyed by shellfire. Carry straight on into Hollebeke, passing under a pylon line and head directly for the church. Look for signs to Voormezele and Golf. Leave the church **(2)** on your immediate right and head west out of the village. By a road junction one kilometre along this road is a memorial by a crossroads to the first deployment of Indian army troops in the area **(3)**. Turn right at the next junction, leaving a small redbrick house on your left and head towards a wooded area. At a right angled bend to the left is a pair of gates. These led into an area known as The Stables. Follow the road (signed Golf) past the main entrance to the golf course to another right angled bend to

The Indian Army memorial near Hollebeke.

the left, where you turn right. Before you do so, look to the left, towards **(4)**, the site of Eikhof Farm. This was the area of some robust fighting on 1 November and a temporary abandonment of the line by French troops.

Proceed down a straight, minor road with various signs, including 'Golfers 50 metres'. At a junction (straight on is barred to vehicles and so

Panoramic Sketch of the Eikhof area by Bavarian Field Artillery Regiment 11 4th Bavarian Infantry Division.

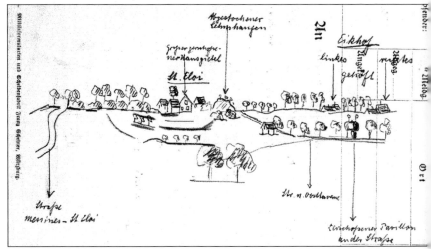

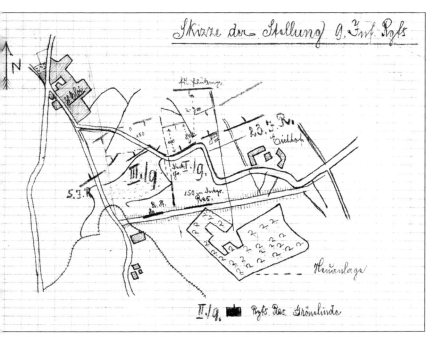

Situation Bavarian Infantry Regiment 9, 4th Bavarian Infantry Division near Eickhof (or Eikhof) Farm, November 1914.

you will bear sharply left), get off the road as best you can. There is a memorial stone **(5)** on the right to the pre war French owners of a huge edifice, known as the White Chateau, who were killed during the war. The chateau and its grounds have entirely disappeared; the modern day golf course has been created on the site of both. The presence of two chateaux in Hollebeke has caused identification problems – the site of the first one being east of the railway line (which often appears in accounts in the early days of the battle) and this one some distance to the west of Hollebeke and near the line of the Comines Canal.

On 2 November, when the main battle had moved on, German cavalry units that had spent the past few days in reserve near to the Lys, were called forward, dismounted, to occupy and improve the trenches near here. A member of Husaren Regiment 3 recalled the scene:

Thirty minutes later we set off [from south of Hollebeke]. *The way was littered with dead horses and shattered ammunition wagons. The nearer we*

The memorial to the two pre war owners of the White Chateau.

193

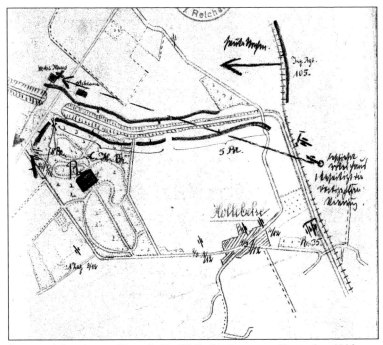

German defensive positions in the White Chateau area, November 1914.

got to the front, the greater the number of shell holes in the road. Hollebeke village! The ghostly outlines of the ruined walls of the monastery stuck up into the night sky. A Red Cross flag waved above a relatively intact; wounded men lay on stretchers before the main door. Now and then there were bursts of small arms fire; the artillery fire slackened off and then stopped entirely. The great chateau was located about two kilometres the far side of the village. The wrecked iron gates of the park hung in shreds from their hinges. On the broad driveway lay one shell splinter after another and several mature old trees had been splintered by shells. In the early dawn the white mass of the chateau could be seen, as could the effect of the heavy shells on it.

From here it is possible to walk forward to the low ground where successive unsuccessful attempts were made prior to the Great War to tunnel under or bridge over the Ypres-Comines canal **(6)**. The business of the tunnel under the canal; there are several references to the tunnel in the *OH* and some regimental accounts, but none of the modern interpretation panels for the canal make any reference at all to it. This area is now given over to recreation and there are numerous explanatory plaques on both sides of the abandoned canal to its construction and the events of 1914-18.

194

The White Chateau in its pre war splendour.

The destroyed White
Chateau (C) and the
collapsed bridge over the
canal (B) later in the war.

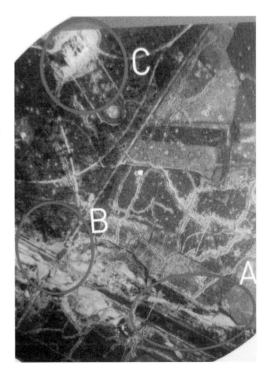

Oak Dump Cemetery.

Return to your vehicle and continue along the road now named Bernikkewallestraat. The road bears right and then left to Oak Dump Cemetery **(7)**, a beautifully landscaped and maintained cemetery with two burials from 1914. Continue along the road and bear left at a junction after about one kilometre then left again at a junction with the N336 (fast moving traffic – care!) Carry on to the roundabout in St Elooi and take the exit towards Armentières. It is also signed to Oosttaverne Cemetery. On the right is the slightly wooded broken country from where the Bavarians launched the assault on Wijtschate. Just before Oosttaverne Cemetery and the memorial to the 19th (Western) Division turn left by a white walled building onto Hollebekestraat, signed Hollebeke 3. Follow the road straight on across two minor crossroads and ignore a couple of turns to the right, heading for Hollebeke church. Note, as you get closer to Hollebeke, that in the fields over to the right **(8)** is the scene of the VC action of Sepoy Khudadad Khan, 129th Baluchis, on 30/31 October. To him belongs the distinction of being the first native winner of the VC of the Indian Army on the Western Front. The tour ends in the centre of Hollebeke village

Tour Nine:

Circuit of Zwarteleen and Klein Zillebeke

See also maps on pp. 125, 138 and 143 and text pp. 126–129 and 141–144.

This tour takes in the Zwarteleen, Klein Zillebeke and Hill 60 areas where the stalemated lines of battle solidified in mid-November 1914 and also includes Zillebeke itself.

Leave the village of Hollebeke, heading north along the road to Zillebeke, crossing the line of the abandoned Ypres - Comines canal **(1)**, where the road bears round to the left and climbs gently away. There is limited car parking on both sides of the canal bridge and walks along the old canal line here; plenty of traces of the war remaining on the ground. It is clear what an obstacle to effective communications that the railway embankment provided in the fighting towards the end of October 1914. The ground on the north side (mainly) of the canal is now open to the

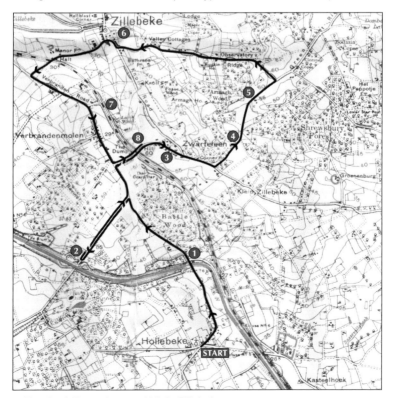

A Circuit of Zwarteleen and Klein Zillebeke.

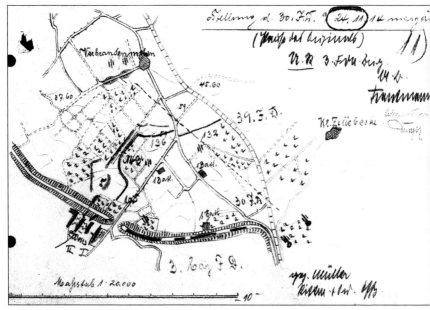

Situation in the Klein Zillebeke area of 30th Infantry Division, 24 November.

public and there are considerable traces of the war remaining, which include the area known as the Bluff.

As you proceed, the ground on either side of the road witnessed considerable fighting in the first weeks of November and beyond, when the intensity of the fighting in the Salient generally died down. [After a while, off to the left, is a road down to De Palingbeek, for those who wish to visit the northern bank of the abandoned canal; there is plenty of parking and there are some explanatory stands with then and now photographs, tracing the ill fated attempts to build the canal and an associated bridge and its fate during the war. For the reasonably fit and able, there are steps leading down the steep bank into the bed of the canal. There is a rather expensive café/restaurant at the end of the road for those who are seeking refreshment **(2)**. On your return journey to the main road, look over to your right, where there were some some bitterly contested actions involving the Germans and the French in the later stages of First Ypres.]

Turn right at the well signposted turn off to Hill 60 and proceed past it; the tour will end at Hill 60, giving plenty of time to explore as desired later on. There are major works going on at Hill 60 (spring 2015), desirable or not depending on viewpoint, which may affect to a small degree the traffic flows, but the directions should remain clear enough. After the café on the left the road forks – take the left hand one and, at the junction turn right, in the direction of Zandvoorde. This is the area of Zwarte Leen **(3)** and a short distance further on, Klein Zillebeke. There is very little to distinguish the boundaries between the two places.

198

All of this area witnessed fierce local actions for much of November, characterised by confused fighting in the woods and furious attempts to capture or retain Hill 60 itself. The British defenders here at various stages in the fighting included several cavalry regiments fighting as infantry. However, because of their mounted capability, they could be moved about the battlefield relatively rapidly, making them a most useful asset. Amongst those to fall at a particularly difficult period for the allies at Klein Zillebeke, on 6 November, were Lieutenant Wyndham and Lieutenant Colonel Wilson (RHG), both buried in Zillebeke Churchyard. On that same day the indefatigable General Moussy, in person and with a drawn sword, led his few reserves in a counter attack to the immediate east of Hill 60. Moussy had enough fame for his action to be quoted by John Buchan in his post war novel novel *Mr Standfast*. This is perhaps also an opportune moment to remind readers of the extent of the French involvement in the fighting at First Ypres, which often gets overlooked. In early November all the ground that you have been covering in this tour was defended by French troops; Hill 60 provides a boundary between the two allied armies, with the British effort being concentrated to the north of it.

Take the first left, wooded on the left and opening out to fields after a short distance on the right. As the ground rises there is a farm on the right and, beyond it a lay by with a bus stop and another building on the left. Pull over here **(5)** and look back to the area of the Brown Road **(4)** and to the wooded area to its immediate north and west. More extensively wooded in 1914, this is the area where Captain John Vallentin of 1/S Staffs won a posthumous VC on 7 November and Lieutenant John Dimmer of 2/KRRC his VC on 12 November.

At the road junction with Green Jacket Ride turn left and head in to Zillebeke. Proceed to the church at Zillebeke **(6)** – plenty of parking nearby – and visit the well known cemetery there, now often described as the Aristocrats Cemetery. A first rate book on this has been written by Jerry Murland, *Aristocrats go to war; uncovering the Zillebeke Cemetery*, providing a useful overview of First Ypres as well as a detailed look at the men who are buried here, including the high proportion of the twenty six identified casualties who were killed in that battle, amongst them Wyndham and Wilson.

Retrace your route from the church and turn left at the T junction, cross the railway line and turn left at the next T junction (noting the British equipped demarcation stone, theoretically marking the limit of the German advance during the war, on the little traffic island in the centre of the road on your left). Pass a turning on the right, signposted to various CWGC cemeteries and look for a turning on the left a couple of hundred metres beyond that, sign posted Larch Wood Cemetery. The approach track to the cemetery is rough but quite drivable, though space to turn around, over the railway crossing, is restricted and could be difficult in very wet weather.

KNOWN TO BE BURIED
IN THIS CEMETERY

FIRST LIFE GUARDS

LIEUTENANT THE HONBLE
WILLIAM REGINALD WYNDHAM
1ST LIFE GUARDS
6TH NOVEMBER 1914 AGE 38

LATE CAPT. 17 LANCERS
JOINED LIFE GUARDS AUG. 1914
KILLED IN ACTION

TO·THE·DEAR·MEMORY·OF
JOHN·H·G·LEE·STEERE
LIEUT·2ND BATTN·GRENADIER
GUARDS·ONLY·CHILD·OF
H·C·LEE·STEERE OF JAYES
HE·FELL·IN·ACTION·NEAR
ZILLEBEKE·17TH NOV·1914
AGED·19·YEARS

HE·ASKED·LIFE·OF·THEE

Renovation work in the cemetery being carried out by workmen of the CWGC.

View from Larch Wood cemetery towards the twin, artificially created, heights of Hill 60 (centre) and the Caterpillar (right).

There are reasonable views from the area of the War Stone towards Hill 60 to the south, to Zwarte Leen to the south east and Verbrande Molen to the south west. Buried in this cemetery is Lieutenant John Eden of 12/Lancers, who was killed on 17 October and buried at the time at Amerika, a hamlet south of Kruiseke. His body, along with two others, was concentrated here after the war; interestingly, the remaining two British burials in that cemetery, both unidentified, were taken for burial to Zandtvoorde (V H 13 and 14). The family contributed significantly to the rebuilding of the church in Kruiseke, recalled by a prominent plaque to the right of the main entrance to it. John Eden was the brother of Anthony Eden, who also served in the war (in the KRRC) and was to be Foreign Secretary for much of the Second World War and succeeded Churchill as Prime Minister in 1955.

Return to the main road and turn left and after a short distance you will come to the turning on the left for Hill 60.

This concludes the tour. Besides visiting this site and appreciating the view offered over Ypres, there is also a café nearby which serves reasonably priced snacks and meals.

Shells by the approach track to the cemetery, off to the left by the railway line, whose route between Hill 60 and the caterpillar can be clearly seen. The hamlet of Verbrande Molen is just visible on the right.

Messines:
Outline German Order of Battle

Most of the formations involved in the area covered by this book belonged to 'Army Group Fabeck' which was subordinated to Sixth Army, commanded by Crown Prince Rupprecht of Bavaria. The German cavalry forces which operated near Messines in October 1914 were under the overall command of General der Kavallerie von der Marwitz, who was simultaneously Senior Cavalry Commander (HKK) 2.

Headquarters Army Group Fabeck was based on XIII (Royal Württemberg) Corps (General der Infanterie von Fabeck).

XV Corps
30th Infantry Division
60 Infantry Brigade (Infantry Regiments 99 & 143)
85 Infantry Brigade (Infantry Regiments 105 & 136)

39th Infantry Division
61 Infantry Brigade (Infantry Regiments 126 & 132)
82 Infantry Brigade (Infantry Regiments 171 & 172)
Composite Jäger Force from HKK 2, under Major Petersen of Jäger Battalion 10

Bavarian II Corps
3rd Bavarian Infantry Division
5 Bavarian Infantry Brigade (Bavarian Infantry Regiments 22 & 23)
6 Bavarian Infantry Brigade (Bavarian Infantry Regiments 17 & 18)

4th Bavarian Infantry Division
7 Bavarian Infantry Brigade (Bavarian Infantry Regiments 5 & 9)
5 Bavarian Reserve Infantry Brigade (Bavarian Reserve Infantry Regiments 5 & 8)

From 31 October
Elements of 6th Bavarian Reserve Division in a reinforcing role. *viz.*
12 Bavarian Reserve Infantry Brigade (Bavarian Reserve Infantry Regiments 17 & 21 [21 normally subordinated to 14 Bavarian Reserve Infantry Brigade and replacing Bavarian Reserve Infantry Regiment 16 temporarily]

From 1 November
Bavarian Reserve Infantry Regiment 20 (14 Bavarian Reserve Infantry Brigade), subordinated with Bavarian Reserve Infantry Regiment 8 to 12 Bavarian Reserve Infantry Brigade to renew assault on Wytschaete.

From 30 October
26th Infantry Division
51 Infantry Brigade (Grenadier Regiment 119 & Infantry Regiment125)
52 Infantry Brigade (Infantry Regiment 121 & Füsilier Regiment 122)

From 3 November
Elements of 3rd Infantry Division in a reinforcing role
5 Infantry Brigade (Grenadier Regiments 2 & 9)

Selective Bibliography

Anglesey, Marquess of: *A History of the British Cavalry Vol 7*. Leo Cooper, 1996

Anon: *War Diary of the 1st Life Guards*

Anon: *List of British Officers Taken Prisoner in the various Theatres of War between August, 1914, and November, 1918*. Cox and Co, 1919

Anon: *Sir John French's Despatches*. London, The Graphic, n.d.

Anon: *Ypres 1914*, Battery Press, n.d.

Astill, E (ed): *The Great War Diaries of Brigadier General Alexander Johnston, 1914 – 1917*, Pen and Sword, 2007

Bickersteth, JB: *History of the 6th Cavalry Brigade.* Baynard Press, n.d.

Bilton, D: *Images of War, The Germans in Flanders 1914*. Pen and Sword, 2012

Brice, Beatrice: *The Battle Book of Ypres*. John Murray 1927

Lloyd, RA: *A Trooper in the Tin Hats*. Naval and Military Press, n.d. (also printed as *Troop Horse and Trench*)

Carnock, Lord: *The History of the 15th The King's Hussars*. Naval & Military Press, n.d.

Congreve, Billy: *Armageddon Road – A VC's Diary 1914 – 1916*, William Kimber, 1982

Connell, J: Wavell, *Scholar and Soldier (to June 1941*. Collins, 1964

Coombs, REB: *Before Endeavours Fade*. After the Battle, 2010 [13th Edition]

Corrigan, G: *Sepoys in the Trenches*. Spellmount, 1999

Darling, JC: *20th Hussars in the Great War*. (Privately) 1923

Davies, F and Maddocks, G: *Bloody Red Tabs*. Pen and Sword, 1995

Edmonds, JE: *Military Operations France and Belgium Vols 1 and 2*. Macmillan and Co., 1922 and 1929

Evans, HKD: *The 4th (Queen's Own) Hussars in the Great War*, Naval & Military Press, n.d.

Farrar-Hockley, A: *Death of an Army*. Worsworth Editions, 1998

Gliddon, G: *VCs of the First World War – 1914*. Alan Sutton 1994

Jourdain, HFN and Fraser, E: *The Connaught Rangers Volume I*. Naval & Military Press, n.d.

Harris, JP: *Douglas Haig and the First World War*. CUP, 2008

Horn, T: *Lancer Dig In*. Ellisons' Edition, 1983

Keith-Falconer, A: *The Oxfordshire Hussars*. John Murray, 1927

Langford, W: *The Great War Illustrated: 1914*, Pen & Sword, 2014

Lindsay, JH: *The London Scottish in the Great War*. Regimental HQ, 1926

Lucy, JF: *There's a Devil in the Drum*. Naval & Military Press, 1993

Lumley, LR: *History of the Eleventh Hussars*. RUSI, 1936

Maze, P: *A Frenchman in Khaki*, William Heinemann, 1934

Mead, G: *The Good Soldier: The Biography of Douglas Haig*. Atlantic Books, 2007

Merewether, JWB and Smith, FS: *The Indian Corps in France*. John Murray, 1918

Oldfield,P: *Victoria Crosses on the Western Front: August 1914 – April 1915, Mons to Hill 60*, Pen & Sword, 2014

Pulteney, W and Brice, B: *The Immortal Salient*, John Murray, 1925

Roynon, G: *The Crofton Diaries Ypres 1914 – 1915*. Sutton, 2004

Sheffield, G: *The Chief – Douglas Haig and the British Army*. Aurum, 2011

Sheldon, J: *The German Army in Ypres, 1914*. Pen and Sword, 2010

Simpson, K: *The Old Contemptibles*. George Allen and Unwin, 1981

Terraine, J: *Douglas Haig: The Educated Soldier*, Hutchinson, 1963

Willcox, WT: *The 3rd (King's Own) Hussars*. John Murray, 1925

Selective Index

213